The **PocketScroll**® Series

SHAAR PRESS

RABBI
ABRAHAM J.
TWERSKI, M.D.

published by

PocketScroll

SHAAR PRESS

Letters to My Children

Table of Contents

Letters to My Children

Introduction: Letters To My Children

It is a great *chesed* from G-d that most of us live fulfilling albeit imperfect lives. Yes, it is true that we are not always blissfully happy and at times we are not on our best behavior. But as Jews we strive to do our very best and, by and large, we succeed. Admittedly, there are numerous bumps in the road and we don't always navigate them optimally, but given the personalities and talents we have, we do the best we can and the results are rewarding. Most of us marry and have children, take care of our responsibilities, and cherish our good fortune to have been born into the Jewish nation.

That being said, good books rarely focus on the happily-ever-after aspect of our daily existence and so, in this volume, I will attempt to address those aspects that may negatively impact us, and I will provide tools to enhance our interactions with those nearest and dearest to us — our families. It is widely assumed that many of our problems are the outcome of difficult childhood experiences: illness, economic deprivation, faulty parenting, and other stress or trauma that have impacted our emotions and resulted in a variety of psychological problems. There is certainly much truth to this, because in childhood we are very impressionable. Events and actions that might not affect an adult can have lasting effects on a child.

But let us consider for a moment. The world was a paradise, *Gan Eden*, and would have remained so if not for the sin of Adam and Eve. But what caused them to err? They had no childhood trauma or deprivation, and certainly no faulty parenting. They were misled to disobey Hashem by the *yetzer hara*. According to the Midrash, Adam was exceedingly great; that Adam nevertheless could have been duped by the *yetzer hara* is an indication of its extraordinary power. The *yetzer hara* can delude people, cause them to fantasize, and distort their perception of reality.

We do not live in *Gan Eden*. Unfortunately, many young people are not adequately prepared for marriage and for parenting. They do the best they can, but that may not be good enough, resulting in faulty parenting that may lead to psychological and physical trauma. But that is not the whole story. It is so evident that childhood experience can affect us as adults that we blame only those experiences and neglect to realize that, like Adam and Eve, we are also subject to the destructive force of the *yetzer hara*.

We may think that by observing Torah and mitzvos we have successfully defeated the *yetzer hara*. We may think that if we have resisted the *yetzer hara's* temptations to sin, we have eliminated it as a cause of our problems, and thus the only remaining cause must be our toxic childhood experiences.

We know that the *yetzer hara* drives us to commit sins, and we believe we are fully aware of its tricks and can defend ourselves. We may not realize that the *yetzer hara* is wily and sinister, and over and above tempting us to sin, it seeks to disable us by undermining our self-esteem and self-confidence.

Gathering material from Torah literature and psychologic sources, I wish to make people aware of the *yetzer hara's* tactics to depress us and make us feel unworthy, and hope to teach us how to protect ourselves from its ruinous influence.

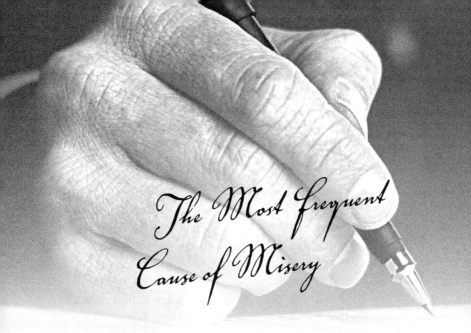

The Most Frequent Cause of Misery

You've been feeling stressed out and depressed. Things are not going well for you at work. Your marriage has some very rough spots. Your relationship with the kids is mediocre. You have great difficulty trying to make decisions. You think of yourself as a failure. You decide to consult a psychotherapist. Here are a few scenarios you might share with the therapist who takes your history.

Your father was a very demanding, irritable person. He did not actually physically abuse you, but he was always critical of you. Nothing you did was ever good enough. You remember him saying, "Can't you ever do anything right?" and that remark went straight to your core. Yes, you loved him because he was your father, and there were ways in which you respected him, but you feel he hurt you deeply. Your mother did not stand up for you to protect you from your father's irascibility. You know that he did not mean to hurt you and she did not mean to abandon you. He was not really a cruel person, but you resented how he acted toward you, and you resent your mother's neutral stance.

You always felt second best or worse in the family. It was a family joke, "Esther, you were supposed to be a boy." "Why can't you be like your sister? She's so pretty and smart!" Your older sister was two years your senior, and was very bright and popular. It was obvious that your mother favored her. You feel, *Why didn't G-d make me a boy? Why wasn't I given a chance to be myself? Why do I have to compete with my sister for attention and approval?*

When you were 5 years old, your mother became seriously ill, and you were placed with an aunt, who grudgingly accepted you. You spent two very miserable months with her. When you returned home, your mother was still not well and there was much anxiety about her health. You felt it was your fault that she was not getting better.

One does not have to be a psychological genius to recognize that the situations you faced, along with the attitudes you felt in your childhood, when your personality was being formed, could have caused you to feel inferior, inadequate, and incompetent. You question whether you deserve to be loved. You don't have high hopes for success. You are unhappy, and you hope that with therapy, you may be able to overcome your negative feelings about yourself and to enjoy life.

You have an excellent therapist. You see him/her once or twice a week. He/she is empathic, and you feel that he/she genuinely cares about you and wants to help you.

You see the therapist regularly for two years, and he/she helps you realize that you are, in fact, a good person, both competent and likable. Your parents were indeed remiss in your upbringing, but that was primarily due to their own psychological issues. When you became an adult, your parents realized that they had not given you a fair deal, and they apologized. The therapist did everything he/she could do to help you overcome your negative childhood experiences and to feel more positive about yourself. To some degree, you do. However, there are still some residual negative feelings. Your therapist tells you that he/she would be happy to continue working with you but that frankly, you have reached a plateau, and that he/she does not see that you could gain much more from continuing therapy.

Now what? Is there no hope that you can achieve the happiness you crave?

Much does indeed depend on the attitudes we experience in our childhood, *but not everything*, and we need to find ways of dealing with those factors that do not respond to therapy. Our self-image —

how we see ourselves — is the major determining factor in whether or not we succeed in life.

I have been accused of having a one-track mind, and I plead guilty as charged. I have indeed said that with the exception of those psychiatric disorders that are of physiologic causation, e.g., bi-polar disorder, all psychological disorders are due, at least in part, and sometimes entirely, to low self-esteem. I feel vindicated by a statement made by the eminent *mussar* (self-improvement) authority, R' Shlomo Wolbe (*Alei Shur,* Vol. 1, p. 168). This brief statement is far reaching.

The Hebrew word for self-esteem is *chashivus,* which means *importance* or *value.* R' Wolbe says, "Without an awareness of *chashivus,* there is no *avodah* (service of Hashem) in Torah."

This is an amazing, challenging statement. R' Wolbe supports his statement by quoting the words we find before and after the giving of the Torah at Sinai. As a precursor to the giving of the Torah, Hashem said to the Israelites, "You shall be unto Me a kingdom of Kohanim," which Rashi translates as *sarim,* officers or ministers, of great status and with great responsibilities (*Exodus* 19:6). After the giving of the Torah, when the Israelites were awestruck hearing the voice of Hashem, Moses said, "Do not fear, for in order to elevate you has Hashem come" (ibid. 20:17).

R' Wolbe says that before and after the giving of the Torah, Hashem stressed the lofty status of every single Jew. "With a feeling of insignificance, one cannot achieve the intent of Torah." One must have a sense of personal *chashivus.*

People have the mistaken impression that because *mussar* requires that a person be aware of one's shortcomings and sins, it is depressing. R' Wolbe cites the *Chovos HaLevavos,* pointing out that before one can do a soul-searching to discover one's character defects, one must feel that one is precious, because one would exert great caution to avoid damaging something that is very valuable. He cites R' Yeruchem Levovitz, the Mirrer Mashgiach, who said, "A person must indeed know his shortcomings so that he knows how to improve on them, but he cannot do so unless he is aware of his character strengths, [knowing] that he is indeed capable of rectifying [his faults]."

The Talmud states, "Every person is *obligated* to say, 'The world was created for me'" (*Sanhedrin* 37a). This is not an expression of vanity or of inflated importance. Rather, it is the awareness that Hashem created the world for a purpose, and *it is the individual's responsibility to see that this purpose is realized.*

The great sage Hillel said, "If I am here, then all is here" (*Succah* 53a). Hillel is noted for his outstanding *anivus* (humility). His statement was not one of grandiosity, but rather of the sense of *chashivus* that is essential for proper living and Torah observance.

I can testify on the basis of fifty years of psychiatric practice that many, many people lack this vital sense of *chashivus.* If you are familiar with some of my writings, you know that I place great emphasis on the problem of *low self-esteem.* By that I mean that some people have *totally unwarranted and unjustified feelings of inferiority.* The reality is that although they may be bright, handsome, capable, and likable, they do not always feel this about themselves. Often they think that they are dull, unattractive, incompetent, and unlikable. Inasmuch as this is not true, they are living and acting according to false premises, and this error may cause many emotional problems. I came to this awareness because of the following experience.

Let me share my personal experience. I had been a rabbi for ten years and a psychiatrist for eight years. I was absolutely certain that my self-concept was accurate. I did not think that I lacked a sense of *chashivus* until "the incident of the whirlpool" shocked me into reality.

I was the medical director of a 300-bed psychiatric hospital, which had the only emergency service in an area of four million people. If a nurse could not reach the patient's private doctor, I would be called. Family members called, as did social workers, lawyers, and probation officers. On a quiet night, I might receive four calls from the emergency room; on a busy night, I took ten calls. I was on constant call.

When my two-week vacation came around, I told my wife that I needed absolute rest: no sight-seeing, no adventures. I wanted to sit on an easy chair in a dimly lit room and simply breathe. No activities. I nixed many vacation sites because they were too busy, and I settled on Hot Springs, Arkansas, because there was no activity there. The industry of Hot Springs is horse racing, and the racing season begins on February 15. If one arrives there before February 7, it is a ghost town. In December I arrived at a town where all the stores were boarded up. Just what I needed.

Having had chronic low-back pain for years, I took advantage of the miraculous mineral baths. An attendant ushered me into a cubicle where I immersed myself in a whirlpool bath. This was paradise! I was not available by telephone. No one could reach me. I had the absolute peace and quiet I had been craving.

After about five minutes, I emerged, thanking the attendant for this heavenly experience. "Where are you going?" the attendant asked.

"I don't know," I replied. "What's next in the treatment?"

The attendant said that in order to continue with the treatment, I must remain in the whirlpool for twenty-five minutes.

I returned to the tub, but after five minutes, I said, "Look, I have to get out of here."

The attendant said, "In that case, you can't go on with the treatment."

Unwilling to forfeit the treatment, I returned to the tub for fifteen minutes of misery.

This was a rude awakening. I had been able to tolerate unrelenting stress at the hospital for three years, but I could not tolerate the peace of paradise for more than a few minutes. Obviously, something was drastically wrong.

I consulted a wise psychologist, who said, "If you ask people how they relax, they may say by reading a book, doing needlework, listening to music, watching videos, playing golf, etc. All of these are diversions, not relaxation. True relaxation is an absence of all activity.

"In your whirlpool, you were deprived of all possible diversions. There was nothing to read, nothing to watch, nothing to listen to, and no one to talk to. Being stripped of all diversions, you were left in the immediate company of yourself. You were alone in a tiny room with *someone you don't like very much*. No wonder you were miserable."

This rang true, and I began to do a soul-searching to find

what was so appalling about me that I could not stand my own presence. I gradually realized that my self-concept was seriously flawed, and I embarked on a journey to discover my real self. That I was successful is evident from the fact that I have been back to Hot Springs several times, and I enjoy a full twenty-five-minute peaceful whirlpool.

I cannot stress the following statement enough: ***If a person's self-concept is negative, that is his reality.*** It is much more than just feeling negative about oneself. He believes that everyone in the world sees him as the negative creature he believes himself to be. If one sees a pile of trash, one believes that everyone looking at it will see a pile of trash, rather than a beautiful rosebush. A person with a negative self-image will believe that everyone will react to him as the inadequate and unworthy person he considers himself to be. Consequently, *he will react to everyone in the world according to his assumption that he is an inferior being.* The fallout of this delusion of inferiority is legion. It affects how one relates to everyone: spouse, parents, children, siblings, friends, employers, etc.

I did not absorb this precious insight from a psychology text, but from a comment by the *Chiddushei HaRim.* When the spies Moses sent to scout Canaan returned, they said that the land was inhabited by a race of giants. "We were like grasshoppers in our eyes, and so we were in their eyes" (*Numbers* 13:33). The *Chiddushei HaRim* states, "The way you feel about yourself is how you believe others see you." This is an important insight and vital to understanding how low self-esteem can damage one's relationships and limit one's happiness.

The Importance of Chashivus

The Baal Shem Tov rhetorically asks, "Inasmuch as *ga'avah* (vanity; arrogance) is a loathsome trait, why did Hashem create it? Everything in creation must have some positive function. Of what possible good is *ga'avah*?" Then he provides the answer. "A person should think so highly of himself that he will not do anything that is beneath his dignity." When the *yetzer hara* wishes to lead a person to sin, it may say, "Go ahead and do whatever pleases you. It doesn't make any difference to anyone." One's response should be, "I'm too proud to do that."

The Talmud says that a person should think of himself as being in a delicate balance, with precisely the same amount of mitzvos and *aveiros.* Inasmuch as a person is judged by the majority of one's actions, if one does one more mitzvah, that tips the scale to the positive side and one is judged a *tzaddik.* If one does one more *aveirah* (sin), that tips the scale to the negative side and one is judged a *rasha*.

Furthermore, a person should think of the world as being comprised of an equal number of *tzaddikim* and *reshaim* (wicked people). If a person does one more mitzvah, that action will give him the status of a *tzaddik*, which will now tip the balance of the world toward the positive, and the world will earn a favorable judgment. If one does one *aveirah*, one will be judged a *rasha*, tipping the world toward the negative, resulting in a harsh judgment (*Kiddushin* 40b).

A person should have a sense of *chashivus* to realize, "The future of the world depends on me." This is the positive application of *ga'avah*.

With low self-esteem, a person cannot have a true sense of the impact he has on the world.

Origin of Low Self-Esteem

A s was noted, we generally attribute low self-esteem to childhood experiences, especially how one was treated by one's parents. It is certainly true that some parents lack good parenting techniques, and even with the best of intentions they may act in ways that cause a child to feel bad about himself. But try as I might, I could not find anything in my childhood to explain why I felt so poorly about myself. My parents were loving and caring. I do not recall any childhood trauma. I succeeded in everything I did. I was a chess champion at ten. I graduated high school at 16, received *semichah* (rabbinic ordination) at 21. I graduated medical school with honors. Yet, I was unhappy with myself, and in spite of my achievements, I lacked self-confidence.

Furthermore, in my many years of psychiatric practice, I could not find anyone who did not have, in one way or another, some unwarranted and unjustified feelings of inadequacy and low self-worth. It seemed to me to be ubiquitous, and the universality of it could not be explained by the commonly assumed cause of parental inadequacy.

This remained an unsolved mystery to me until fairly recently, when I came across a statement by the *mussar* authority, R' Simchah Zissel Ziv, who commented on the verse in *Psalms* (118:13), "*Dacho dechisani linpol, vaHashem azarani*, They pushed me hard that I might fall, but Hashem assisted me.*" R' Simchah Zissel makes this amazing statement. Referring to the duplicate usage, *dacho dechisani*, he says, "*Dacho* is not a verb. Rather, *dacho* is a noun, and refers to the crushing force *that is inherent in human nature, which tries to topple a person to the ground by making one feel worthless.*" This force of lowliness that is inherent in man's nature pressures him with great power. Inasmuch as it is inherent in man's nature, it affects all human beings, even those who are fortunate to have had excellent parenting and a happy childhood. King David is saying that this all-encompassing force, which has such great power, can totally crush a person, and if not for Hashem's assistance, a person would be unable to withstand this crushing force (*Chochmah U'Mussar*, Vol. 3, p. 113).

When I read this, a bright light went on in my mind. This can explain the prevalence of negative feelings about oneself, which may be totally contradictory to one's reality. It explains why people who did not have negative childhood experiences and who may be successful in everything they do, may nevertheless have low self-esteem. Even competent therapy may not resolve the problem.

This force, which seeks to crush a person, is none other than the *yetzer hara,* the evil instinct, which exists in every person. R' Simchah Zissel is actually elaborating on the passage in the Talmud, "A person's *yetzer* renews itself every day ... and seeks to kill him"

(*Kiddushin* 30b). This explains why, although I had an ideal childhood and wonderful parents, I developed severe negative feelings about myself. It was the working of the *yetzer hara*.

The Talmud says that we acquire the *yetzer hara* at birth, but we do not acquire the *yetzer tov* until we reach the stage of bar mitzvah or bas mitzvah. This means that the crushing and depressing force of the *yetzer hara* was unopposed for 12 or 13 years! No wonder that so many people feel inferior and inadequate. For so many years, the internal voice was telling them how no-good they are, and there was no positive inner voice to contradict it. If we become aware of having low self-esteem and want to change how we feel about ourselves, it is an uphill fight to undo all the negativity that we were fed for more than a decade.

The cause of low self-esteem as an effect of the *yetzer hara* explains a phenomenon that has eluded self-esteem psychologists; namely, the "self-esteem paradox." We often find that people who are gifted tend to have a lower self-esteem than people who are less blessed.

Inasmuch as low self-esteem is the work of the *yetzer hara*, we can understand this. The Talmud says that the greater a person, the greater is his *yetzer hara* (*Succah* 52a). Hashem will not give a person of limited capabilities a strong *yetzer hara* that would overwhelm him. King Solomon implies that Hashem has made the good and evil inclinations equal to each other in intensity (*Ecclesiastes* 7:14). A person with greater potential strength will be given a proportionally greater *yetzer hara*. Hence, people who are gifted with more potential have a greater force that seeks to crush them.

We generally think that the *yetzer hara* tempts people to do forbidden things. That is indeed true. But even more important is what R'

Simchah Zissel points out: The *yetzer hara* seeks to crush a person and make one feel insignificant and unworthy.

R' Aharon of Karlin tells us that nowhere does the Torah say that *atzvus* (depression) is an *aveirah*. However, there are few traits that can result in so many *aveiros* as *atzvus*, a feeling of unworthiness and insignificance. If the *yetzer hara* succeeds in making a person commit a sin, it has had a partial success. If it succeeds in throwing a person into a feeling of *atzvus*, it has made a major triumph. It is like the difference between extinguishing a single light and shutting off the main power to the entire house.

This is not to deny the important impact parents can have on a child's self-esteem and emotional well-being. Certainly, if there have been errors in parenting, every attempt should be made in therapy to reduce and, if possible, eliminate the noxious effects. However, parenting errors and other childhood experiences are not the entire story. The role of the *yetzer hara* should be taken into account.

The problem is that if a therapist assumes that *all* of a person's problems are the result of faulty parenting, this skews the therapist's objectivity to the client's reality. It is as if the therapist has reached a foregone conclusion, "You must have been messed up by your parents. Let's look into your history and find just what they did." With this approach, one can find mistakes in all parents, because no human being is perfect.

I have seen instances where the therapeutic approach of blaming the parents has turned a child against the parents, alienating the very people who care most about the person. The premise that early life experiences are entirely responsible for problems in adulthood carries with it the risk of unjustly faulting the parents.

Furthermore, if the parents are seen as the sole or primary cause of a person's low self-esteem or other psychological problems and the role of the *yetzer hara* is overlooked, no steps will be taken to neutralize the effect of the *yetzer hara*. If a therapist feels that the latter is not his role but is the proper territory of a spiritual mentor, the therapist can make a referral to the latter. If the effect of the *yetzer hara* is not taken into account, one can be in never-ending therapy and still not be free of emotional distress.

The following challenging statement appeared in *Psychotherapy Networker,* Vol. 39 #2 (March/April 2015).

> Perhaps the most enduring but unsubstantiated theoretical belief among therapists is the timeworn notion that difficulties in adulthood stem from childhood misfortunes. Almost all therapy approaches, from psychoanalysis and Imago therapy to the emotion-focused and sensorimotor methods, embrace some version of this dogma. Given its venerable pedigree, this belief in the potency of childhood events is one of the most difficult to deconstruct. Nevertheless, as a general clinical hypothesis, it's deeply flawed.
>
> The simple truth is that a preponderance of the evidence mitigates against assigning any great importance to childhood experiences and memories: processed, unprocessed, or reprocessed. Martin Seligman, the former president of the American Psychological Association, puts it this way: "Childhood events — even childhood trauma — and childrearing appear to have only weak effects on

adult life. Childhood, contrary to popular belief, does not seem, empirically, to be particularly formative. **So, contrary to popular belief, we are not prisoners of our past.**" [Emphasis added.]

Debunking this time-hallowed theory is akin to rejecting the beliefs that the earth is flat and that the sun rotates around the earth. After all, it is obvious that the sun rises in the east and sets in the west as it travels around the earth. When Copernicus asserted that the earth revolves around the sun rather than the reverse, he was soundly denounced. His religious authorities declared this theory to be heresy. The notion that our personalities are not determined by our childhood will not fade without a vigorous fight.

One reason the theory that our adult problems are due to our parents is so tenacious is the human propensity to blame. I have often said, only half in jest, that there are four essentials to human life: (1) food and water, (2) clothing, (3) shelter, and (4) *someone to blame.* The reason why the latter is so powerful and ubiquitous is because as long as we can blame someone else, we do not have to accept responsibility and we do not have to make any changes in ourselves. We are creatures of habit and we wish to do things the way we are accustomed to doing them. Furthermore, we do not wish to feel that we are at fault. Finding someone to blame relieves us of this problem, and this propensity may lead to scapegoating the parents. We may be happy feeling sorry for ourselves as innocent victims, but this does nothing to correct the errors in our thinking and behavior.

In light of this, R' Simchah Zissel's statement takes on new and greater importance. If parents are not completely responsible for a person developing low self-esteem, then who is? R' Simchah Zissel states it is the crushing force of the *yetzer hara*. That may be tough to swallow, but unless we realize this fact, we will fail to take effective steps to neutralize the *yetzer hara*.

The awareness that one's low self-esteem may be due to the *yetzer hara*, as R' Simchah Zissel says, has important applications. Neutralizing the effects of the *yetzer hara* is not like taking an antibiotic that eliminates the disease-causing bacteria. Remember the Talmudic statement, "A person's *yetzer* renews itself and grows stronger *every day* and seeks to crush him" (*Kiddushin* 30a). If you succeeded in neutralizing the *yetzer hara* today, you can be sure that it will return tomorrow and use every trick in the book to crush you. It may even masquerade as a *tzaddik* who encourages you to do *teshuvah* (repent; repentance). It may bring up actions from the past for which you did *teshuvah* and attained forgiveness, and it may seek to depress your self-concept by reminding you of your sins, telling you that your *teshuvah* was inadequate, and that you are undeserving of Hashem's love. The struggle to maintain a sense of *chashivus* is ongoing, because the *yetzer hara* is relentless.

The Rebbe of Kotzk warned against this maneuver. We are to believe that once we have done proper *teshuvah*, Hashem has completely erased our sins, as the prophet says, "I have wiped away your willful sins like a cloud and your errors like a mist" (*Isaiah* 44:22). In fact, if we do *teshuvah* out of love for Hashem, our sins are converted into merits (*Yoma* 86b). But the *yetzer hara* will not give up and will tell you that your *teshuvah* was not adequate. It is important to have a competent *talmid chacham* as a mentor who will guide you.

The *yetzer hara* may try to depress you by telling you that there are some deeds for which you cannot do *teshuvah*. For example, you offended someone, and *teshuvah* requires that you apologize and obtain *mechilah* (forgiveness). However this person moved away, and all your efforts to locate him have been futile. It appears that you can never get forgiveness.

Sidduro shel Shabbos says that if you have truly done everything within your power to locate this person to obtain *mechilah*, you can be certain that Hashem will put it in that person's heart to be *moichel* (forgive).

Being aware that your low self-esteem is the work of the *yetzer hara* that seeks to crush and disable you, you are in a position to reject its ideas, just as you reject it when it urges you to eat something *tereifeh* or to violate Shabbos. As *Chovos HaLevavos* says, "You may be asleep, but the *yetzer hara* is always alert," and it seeks to bring you down.

The most serious problem of the *yetzer hara* is that it has the power to convince a person that false is true. An example of how a person can be convinced of a distortion of reality is demonstrable by hypnosis.

> I have demonstrated hypnosis to groups of physicians; one experiment involves asking the hypnotized subject if he would like to eat an orange. If he agrees, I cut a lemon in half and give it to him. The subject eats the lemon and smacks his lips with pleasure while the audience grimaces. After the subject emerges from the trance, he may ask, "Can I have the other half of the orange?" When I show him the lemon, he says, "That's a lemon. I would never eat that."

Just as in hypnosis a person can be deluded to believe that a lemon is an orange, so too, the *yetzer hara* can delude a person and distort one's perception. As King David said, "*Dacho dechisani linpol,* it seeks to topple a person," and we must be on the alert to avoid falling into its trap.

Low Self-Esteem vs. Humility

"There is only a handbreadth between *Gan Eden* and *Gehinnom*," states *Koheles Rabbah* 7:31. Yet they are so vastly different. It might seem that low self-esteem and humility are similar, but there could not be a greater pair of opposites. The *sefarim* say that *anavah* (humility) is the finest of all character traits, and brings one close to Hashem. Low self-esteem, on the other hand, is destructive.

We have defined low self-esteem as being *unwarranted* feelings of inferiority and negativity about oneself. They are delusional feelings of unworthiness, and because they are false, they are *sheker* (falsehood), and *sheker* is evil.

Halachah (Jewish law) provides many precautionary ordinances that are intended to distance a person from committing an *aveirah*; these halachos (laws) are of rabbinic origin. For example, the Torah expressly forbids meat prepared with milk. Many halachos regarding cooking and eating were set down by the Sages to help us avoid inadvertently violating the Scriptural transgression. However, there is only one instance where the Torah directly commands us to distance ourselves from an *aveirah* — and that is *sheker*. "Distance yourself from a false word" (*Exodus* 23:7). Because low self-esteem is *sheker*, it must be assiduously avoided.

Unless one is cautious, one may overstep the bounds of humility and cross the fine line that leads to low self-esteem. A prime example of a person who committed this error is King Saul, whose humility was legendary. When the Israelites were to choose a king by casting lots, Saul the son of Kish was selected, but he was nowhere to be found. Shunning the position of glory, he had "hidden among the baggage" (*I Samuel* 10:21-22).

When the prophet, Samuel, ordered Saul to eradicate Amalek, Saul yielded to the wishes of the populace and took the livestock as booty. He also spared King Agag, whose descendant, Haman, threatened the extinction of all the Jews. Samuel sharply rebuked Saul, "Though you may be small in your own eyes, you are the head of the tribes of Israel" (ibid., 15:17). Saul lost the kingship because of his misguided humility.

In my own generation, we witnessed true greatness and true humility in the person of Rabbi Yisrael Meir Kagan, the Chofetz Chaim (1838-1933). He dressed simply, not in the official garb of a rabbi. He would have been indistinguishable in a crowd. Clearly, the Chofetz Chaim was aware that he knew all of halachah, else he would not have composed the *Mishnah Berurah*, the universally accepted halachah guide.

It is said that in the Chofetz Chaim's generation, the outstanding Talmudic scholars were the Rogatchover Gaon, R' Meir Simchah (*Ohr Samei'ach*); the Rebbe of Gur; the *Avnei Nezer*, R' Chaim Ozer of Vilna, and others; the Chofetz Chaim, although acknowledged as a great *tzaddik*, was generally not thought of as being in the circle of the *geonim*. They say this was because, aware that his knowledge of Torah was encyclopedic, the Chofetz Chaim, in his profound humility, prayed to Hashem that it should not become known. But then, why did he not also pray that he should not be recognized as a great *tzaddik*? Because it simply did not occur to him! Great *tzaddikim* do not think of themselves as *tzaddikim*. Yet, they know their potential greatness and work to actualize it.

We are unaware of the potential greatness within us. In *Sichos Mussar* 5731 #18, R' Chaim Shmulevitz cites the example of the prophet Samuel, whose mother, Chanah, was initially barren and prayed fervently for a child. R' Chaim quotes an opinion in the Talmud, that Chanah's prayer for *zera anashim* was for "an average child," not bright, but not foolish. Chanah later remarked about Samuel, "This is the child that I prayed for," meaning that she had been blessed with exactly what she had prayed for: an average child. Think of it! The prophet Samuel — who our Sages equate with Moses and Aaron — was considered to be just "an average child," not endowed with exceptional abilities!

Low self-esteem does not allow one to assert oneself. A person with low self-esteem is passive to the point of timidity and cannot provide direction, teaching, and leadership when they are necessary. True Torah leaders recognize their own greatness in learning, but do not think of themselves as superior to others.

The feeling of insignificance caused by low self-esteem, which R' Wolbe states is antithetical to Torah observance, is often subconscious, so that a person is not aware of it. Indeed, one may consciously think of oneself as being great. Hundreds of years ago, Rabbeinu Yonah said that a *baal ga'avah*, an arrogant person, actually feels inadequate and inferior, and his inflated self-importance is an escape from those painful feelings of inferiority. The person quashes these feelings by thinking he is superior to others (*Rabbeinu Yonah al haTorah*, p. 156).

How fortunate we are to have known R' Moshe Feinstein, who asserted himself as a leading *posek*, adhering to his halachic convictions even in defiance of opposition. Yet this great *gaon* would frequently read letters sent to an illiterate neighbor, to whom he related with the utmost respect. A *baal ga'avah* would have said, "My time is too precious to give of it to a person who never even learned to read." That is the difference between low self-esteem and humility.

Unconscious Pain

One might think that the term "unconscious pain" is an oxymoron. Pain is a sensation one feels, and if one is not conscious of it, one is not feeling it. But there is some validity to the concept. Some people whose severe pain is relieved by morphine have said, "I still have the sensation, but it does not cause me distress." In other words, it is possible to have pain and not be aware of it.

This is often the case with low self-esteem. Often, one is aware that one feels inferior and lacks self-confidence; this is a most distressing feeling. We have many defense mechanisms, both physical and psychological, and we may be unaware of how they operate. If pathological bacteria enter the body, white blood cells from all parts of the body migrate to the site of the infection to destroy the bacteria. This happens without our being aware of it.

Psychological defenses are no different. In order to spare a person distress, the human mind may employ any number of maneuvers, known as "psychological defense mechanisms." The individual is not aware that these mechanisms are in operation, because they are unconscious.

One of the most common psychological defenses is *denial.* Denial does not mean that one is lying. Lying is conscious, and the liar knows that what is said is not true. Denial is unconscious. The person is unaware of the denial. Here is a classic example of denial.

A 50-year-old woman was admitted to the hospital for exploratory surgery because of a suspected tumor. She told the doctor that she was very active in community affairs and had assumed many important responsibilities. She stated that she was aware that a tumor might mean cancer, and that it was important for her to know the truth, since it would be unfair to many people and many organizations for her to continue carrying responsibilities if her health and ability to function were to deteriorate. The doctor promised to be frank with her and reveal all the surgical findings.

At surgery it was found that she indeed had a cancerous tumor, which was removed. However, because there was indication that the cancer had already spread, she would have to undergo a course of chemotherapy. She expressed her gratitude to the doctor for being truthful with her and said that she would cooperate with whatever treatment was recommended. She spoke freely with the nurses and the staff about her cancer.

The administration of chemotherapy requires intravenous

injection, but this was difficult to do because she had poor veins. Each time she received chemotherapy, multiple attempts to find a vein were necessary. On one occasion, I was called to administer the medication, and luckily, I found a vein on my first try. The patient concluded that I had some unique skill in giving intravenous medication, and requested that I be the one to administer all her medications.

The patient returned weekly for her chemotherapy. She would announce, "I'm here for my cancer shot." She remarked how fortunate she was to be living in an era when science had found a successful treatment for cancer. She appeared to be adjusting well, both physically and emotionally.

Several months after the surgery, she began experiencing joint pain and shortness of breath. The chemotherapy was no longer effective, and she was readmitted to the hospital. She was very angry, and said, "I can't understand you doctors. I've been coming here regularly, and you just haven't been able to find what's wrong with me."

The latter remark was astonishing to me, since she had repeatedly referred to having cancer. It became evident that as long as cancer was something abstract and did not pose an immediate threat to her life, she could accept the diagnosis. Once the condition progressed to the point of causing pain and shortness of breath — concrete evidence that her physical condition was deteriorating — she felt so threatened that her psychological system shut off the realization of the truth. She was not intentionally lying or pretending. At this time, she actually did not believe that she had cancer.

We find an incident of denial in the Torah. When the angel told Abraham that he would have a son, Sarah laughed in disbelief. When Hashem told Abraham that Sarah did not believe that she could bear a child, Abraham reprimanded her. The Torah states, "Sarah denied it, saying, 'I did not laugh,' because she was frightened" (*Genesis* 18:10-15).

Chiddushei HaRim comments, "Heaven forbid that the matriarch Sarah did not have faith in Hashem. Sarah did not lie. Rather, Sarah was *in denial.* Her *yiras Shamayim* was so great that she could not imagine that she had not believed the angel. When she said, 'I did not laugh,' she was telling the truth to the best of her ability."

When an idea is very threatening to a person, the unconscious mind can make one oblivious to it. It is not unusual for people to overlook early signs of a life-threatening illness. Going to the doctor might reveal the dreaded diagnosis, so they simply ignore the warning signs.

The statement cited earlier by Rabbeinu Yonah is an example of denial. The person thinks himself to be superior to others to shield him from the discomfort of feeling inferior.

The major problem of denial is that it is a gross distortion of reality. *One cannot adjust properly to reality if one misperceives it.* The person who overlooks the early signs of cancer pays a terrible price.

Sometimes the denial defense is weak and it tends to fail, in which case the mind adds more defenses to support it. Common among these is *projection*, which consists of attributing what you want to deny about yourself onto someone else. The Talmud's example of this defense mechanism is that of a person who frequently referred to others as being illegitimate; the Talmud concludes that this is reason to consider him as illegitimate. Shmuel says that a person who insults others is projecting his own defects onto them (*Kiddushin* 70a).

The Baal Shem Tov elaborated on this concept, saying that the world is a mirror. Inasmuch as one is often blind to one's own faults, Hashem arranges that one sees them in someone else. Therefore, if you see a fault in someone else, do a careful soul-searching, because you invariably have that fault. If you did not have it, you would not have noticed it in others.

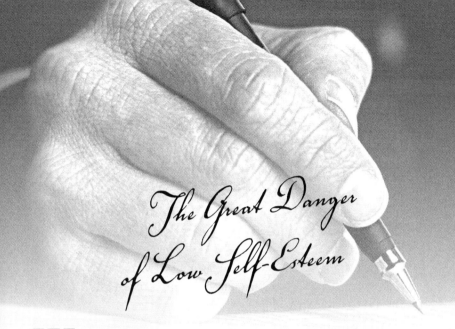

The Great Danger of Low Self-Esteem

When a disease causes symptoms, one can consult a physician for treatment. The danger of cancer is that it is initially silent, and the person is not aware of it. That is also true of low self-esteem. We may not be aware of how a distorted self-image can affect us. It can result in depression, but this is not the type of depression that is relieved with medication.

R' Chaim Shmulevitz cites the incident of the sin of the Golden Calf, whose bitter consequences we still feel today. He asks, "After the Revelation at Sinai, the Israelites were at an extraordinary high level of spirituality. How was it possible for them to have such a precipitous fall to idolatry?"

R' Chaim answers, "Moses had been away for forty days. Satan deluded the Israelites into believing that Moses had died. In fact, he caused them to hallucinate, seeing Moses being carried to his burial. They were in a barren desert, and without Moses, they would not know where to go. Without Moses, they would have no food or water. They panicked! In a state of panic, one loses all ability to make proper judgments, and one may do things that one would never do otherwise."

In its effort to destroy us, to deprive us of our dignity as humans and lower us to an animal level, the *yetzer hara* deludes us and blinds us to our *chashivus*. If we do not believe in ourselves, we can make serious errors in judgment, much as our ancestors did in the desert. We are not aware that our low self-esteem is delusional, and we may act as if in a panic.

The major problem is that we may not be aware that we have low self-esteem. To help recognize this problem, here is a list of some of the more common manifestations:

> ➤ excessive people-pleasing
> ➤ the inability to say "no" when one should
> ➤ sensitivity to criticism
> ➤ seeking to control others
> ➤ procrastination
> ➤ reluctance to advance oneself
> ➤ frequent recourse to alcohol or tranquilizers
> ➤ blaming others when things go wrong
> ➤ denigrating others
> ➤ seeking recognition

If you find yourself acting in these ways, realize that you may be suffering from low self-esteem. It is important to undergo a psychologic evaluation and also to take steps to neutralize the destructive force of the *yetzer hara*.

Escaping the Discomfort of Low Self-Esteem

As I pointed out, I was not aware that I had low self-esteem until the whirlpool incident. Looking back, I can see that much of my behavior was the result of my low self-esteem. I used to seek approval from others to reassure me that I was fine. I used to give sermons every Shabbos, and if people did not approach me to compliment me profusely on the brilliance of my sermon when I alighted from the *bimah*, I felt slighted. I believed that my well-prepared sermon was a failure, and I was miserable for the remainder of that Shabbos. Although I most often did receive praise, the reassurance I garnered from approval by others was short-lived, and I was soon off to seek more approval. I did some rather unusual things to gain approval from others.

I have memories of seeking approval in first grade. It is only normal to want approval and to wish to be appreciated. This becomes a problem when it is overdone, and when failure to receive the desired amount of approval results in resentment and in depression.

> One of my patients was a prominent lawyer who was very active in community affairs. He said, "Doctor, one wall in my home is completely covered with plaques of tribute and honorary testimonials. They mean nothing to me." When he received public recognition, it alleviated his low self-esteem for perhaps a few minutes, but then the delusion of inferiority recurred.

Escaping the discomfort of low self-esteem by any means leaves the basic feelings of inferiority unresolved. It is just like escaping the pain of acute appendicitis by taking a painkiller, which will eliminate the pain but allow the appendicitis to progress until the organ ruptures. The underlying problem must be addressed.

Some people escape the distress of low self-esteem by overachieving. While this may seem innocuous, it is a costly expenditure of energy and may encroach on family life. High achieving is healthy, but overachieving is the defense mechanism of an erroneous self-concept.

A much more serious escape from low self-esteem is the need to wield control. Exercising power over others can indeed provide relief from low self-esteem, but is dangerous. Spouses who wield control, in whatever way, are abusive. They may wish to be loved, but control breeds resentment rather than love.

> I have resentment-filled memories of a fifth-grade teacher who was overly strict to the students, whose response was fear and hatred. In retrospect, I can feel sorry for this woman, who escaped from low self-esteem by exerting her authority over helpless children who had no recourse to her harsh discipline.

Failure is unpleasant, but is unavoidable. Indeed, failure is part of normal life. A baseball player who has a .300 batting average is called out seven out of ten times at bat; this 30 percent success rate commands a salary of millions of dollars.

A person with good self-esteem who fails at something will take the failure in stride, lick his wounds, try to see what went wrong, and try again. Failure is indeed unpleasant, but usually is not catastrophic. To a person with low self-esteem, a failure may be so severe a setback that he will not try again, for fear of another disappointment. I know some very capable people who were hindered from progress in their lives because they could not risk failure. Likewise, a person may resort to perfectionism to avoid failure, but perfectionism inevitably results in failure.

The anxiety about possible failure not only deters people from progress, but may also result in precipitating the very failure one fears. The tension of anticipating the failure may be unbearable, so that one does something to bring about the failure. This is not an uncommon phenomenon. Of course, the failure further depresses the person's already low self-esteem.

Productive criticism is man's best friend, because it enables a person to improve himself. But if you have low self-esteem, even the best-intended criticism is intolerable.

I was asked to participate in a course for addiction therapists at the University of South Carolina. One hundred and ten therapists attended, and a month later, I received a packet of 110 evaluations of my lectures. As I went through them, my ego rose through the ceiling. There were 109 glowing evaluations, but there was one that was critical. My ego fell through the floor. I was depressed for three weeks, until it finally dawned on me that 109 to 1 is not a bad score.

The *yetzer hara* is perfectly happy with the escapist maneuvers noted above, because they can provide a modicum of comfort, diverting attention from one's low self-esteem. The person is left without the feeling of *chashivus* that is so essential to *avodas Hashem*.

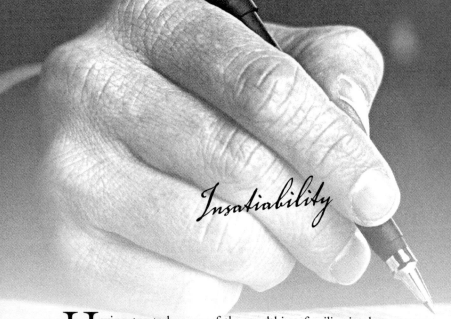

Insatiability

Having treated some of the wealthiest families in the country, I understand the Talmudic statement, "Who is wealthy? One who is satisfied with one's portion" (*Ethics of the Fathers* 4:1).

People with low self-esteem are chronically dissatisfied but do not have the faintest idea why. As noted, they may consult a psychiatrist and be treated with antidepressant medication, which does not relieve their discontent. They may consult a psychotherapist, but if the latter does not address the self-esteem problem, the therapy cannot be completely effective.

Low self-esteem is distressing, but one is unaware that it is the root cause of one's discontent. Naturally, a person will seek ways to relieve the distress. One may seek thrills, pursue wealth or acclaim, denigrate others, have recourse to alcohol or tranquilizers, or do anything that one thinks will make one feel better. All these maneuvers can pro-duce a transient relief, but just as the relief of alcohol wears off after a short while, so it is with any of the other maneuvers. One may be envious or critical of others and angry because one is being deprived of happiness.

It does not dawn on most people that the culprit is the *yetzer hara*, which, by causing them to feel badly about themselves, leads them to negative and destructive traits. They may think that their maneuvers are effective, not recognizing that they provide only short-term relief. Ultimately, they expend themselves in the search for the happiness that continues to elude them.

Many divorces are the result of implicating the marriage as the reason for one's discontent. If the *yetzer hara* succeeds in breaking up a marriage, it has achieved a major triumph, causing ruination not only to the couple, but also to their children.

> *The Talmud relates that a couple who lived near R' Meir's home would argue with each other every Erev Shabbos. R' Meir stayed with them on three consecutive Fridays and restored peace between them.*
>
> *R' Meir heard Satan cry out, "Woe unto me! R' Meir has ejected me from this home" (Gittin 52a).*

If one has sustained a painful injury, treatment can result in long-term relief, because the treatment addressed the cause of the pain. With chronic dissatisfaction, relief through therapy may be of only short duration because the cause, low self-esteem, is not suspected and not addressed.

Seeking Recognition

It is only normal to want recognition. Little children, who may feel lost in the environment of giants, may stand on a chair and say, "Look, Mommy, how big I am."

Like any other psychological trait, the difference between normal and abnormal is quantitative rather than qualitative. Everyone desires recognition, but when this desire is carried to an extreme it becomes problematic. People with low self-esteem are like the child who stands on a chair to appear tall; they have a very strong need to be noticed.

Our *gedolim*, who had true humility, did not call attention to themselves. As noted, the Chofetz Chaim, who did not hold a position as a community rav, saw no need to wear rabbinic garb; unless one knew who he was, one could not pick him out in a crowd. Many *gedolim* were actually in agony because they received public acclaim.

The Tzemach Tzedek of Lubavitch took his young son,
Shmuel, on a journey. When they returned home, the
Tzemach Tzedek found a letter that Shmuel had written
to his mother, in which he said how proud he felt because his
father was receiving such great acclaim.

The Tzemach Tzedek said to Shmuel, "My blood was
being spilled like water, and you enjoyed it?"

The excessive drive for recognition is a telltale sign of low self-esteem, and it is actually self-defeating. The Talmud states this clearly, "He who pursues glory will find that glory eludes him. He who flees from glory will find that glory pursues him" (*Eruvin* 13b).

You may remember the class clown, who got himself kicked out of class every day, and smiled as he left the room. His antics worked, because everyone noticed him.

A man came to the United States after World War II with nothing but the shirt on his back. He was very resourceful, saved his money, invested in real estate, and became very wealthy. He was a philanthropist and a prominent citizen in the community. His son was a very average young man who felt grossly inferior standing in his father's shadow.

I worked for a prison, performing psychiatric evaluations on those who had been arrested. One day, on the list of prisoners whom I was to evaluate I saw the name of this wealthy man's son, who had been arrested in a foiled bank robbery. When they brought him into the office for our session, he extended his hand to shake and smilingly said, "Hey, Rabbi! Did you see my picture in the paper today?"

Indeed, his picture had been on the front page of the newspaper. His need for recognition was so severe that it led him to this criminal behavior, yet he was happy because his photograph had been widely publicized.

If we feel okay about ourselves, we do not need to advertise it. The Talmud says that a single coin in a container will make a great deal of noise if you shake the container. If the container is full of coins, it will make no noise at all when shaken (*Bava Metzia* 85b). If one boasts about oneself, it indicates that one feels impoverished.

"Pseudo" Self-Esteem

People may mistake a feeling for self-esteem, when, in fact, it is just the opposite. True self-esteem is *internal*; one has a feeling of *chashivus*, of being worthy because of *what one is*, rather than by external factors, such as how much money one has, what kind of position of power or authority one occupies, or how impressive a home or car one owns. These external factors actually detract from self-esteem.

Self-esteem means that you have a positive identity that is not dependent on other people's opinions of you. The Rebbe of Kotzk expressed this in his famous statement, "If I am I because I am I, and you are you because you are you, then I am and you are. But, if I am I because you are you, and you are you because I am I, then I am not and you are not." In other words, one's true identity should be independent of what others may think about one.

Among my favorite folk tales are the stories of "the wise men of Chelm." These stories are about a group of villagers who were remarkably foolish in a quaint sort of way. Psychology stresses the importance of having an identity. Psychotherapists often try to help people "find themselves." A popular psychological theme is "Who am I really?" This story of the wise men of Chelm lends a perspective to this issue.

> *One day, a citizen of Chelm was at the public bathhouse. It suddenly dawned upon him that without clothes, most people look somewhat alike. He became quite anxious, thinking, When it comes time to go home, how will I know which one is me?*
>
> *After pondering this for a while, he came up with a brilliant solution. He found a piece of red string and tied it around his great toe. He was now distinctly identifiable.*
>
> *Unfortunately, in the process of sudsing and rinsing, the red string fell off his toe. When another bather stepped on it, it stuck to his foot.*
>
> *When it was time to leave, the first bather looked at his foot, and seeing nothing on his toe, was perplexed. Then he noticed the other man with the string on his foot. He approached him and said, "I know who you are, but can you tell me, who am I?"*

Some people seek an identity by having the equivalent of a red string. Their identity is the luxury automobile in the driveway or the impressive façade on their mansion. But this is hardly an internal identity. What happens if one sells the car? Does the identity go along with it?

It is not much different if one's perception of one's identity is, "I am a doctor" or "I am a lawyer." That is a description of what one *does* rather than what one *is*. If one's only identity is "I am a doctor," then one shares an identity with myriads of other doctors, but one does not have an individual identity.

If one's feeling of *chashivus* is because of being a violin virtuoso, and then unfortunately one suffers from a neurologic condition that makes it impossible to play the violin, one loses the sense of *chashivus*. If one is a great *talmid chacham* who teaches Torah and then suffers a stroke so that one can no longer teach Torah, this is indeed a severe blow to one's ego, but this should not diminish one's sense of *chashivus*. One must uphold the dignity of a Torah scholar who has lost his acuity in Torah. "The broken original Tablets of the Ten Commandments were in the Ark together with the intact Tablets" (*Berachos* 8b).

Perhaps this is what the Talmud means by stating, "If you have studied much Torah, do not take credit for yourself, because that is what you were created to do" (*Ethics of the Fathers* 2:9). The statement is not meant to minimize the value of Torah study. If one has not been blessed with a brilliant mind and an excellent memory, and yet studies Torah to the best of one's ability, one should not feel lesser *chashivus* than one to whom Torah study comes easily.

If one recognizes that one has low self-esteem, then one can take the necessary steps to develop a healthy self-esteem. However, if one has a pseudo self-esteem that is dependent on external factors, one may never realize that one is lacking in true self-esteem. It is much the same as satisfying one's hunger with empty calories. One may not feel hunger, but one may nevertheless remain nutritionally deficient.

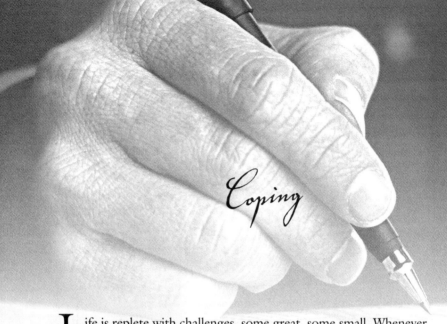

Coping

Life is replete with challenges, some great, some small. Whenever one is confronted with a challenge of any magnitude, there are only two options: cope with the challenge or escape. There is no third option.

How does one decide whether to cope or escape? One assesses the magnitude of the challenge and one's ability to cope. If the challenge is overwhelming, one escapes. If it is within one's ability to cope, one copes. If the two are about equal, one may seek outside assistance in coping.

Escaping is not always wrong. If your car is stuck on the railroad track and you hear a train approaching, you must escape. There is no other way one can cope with a train bearing down at full speed. However, most of life's challenges are not trains and are well within

one's ability to cope. But if one suffers from low sel
think oneself unable to cope.

Choosing to escape from challenges that are with
skills is a serious mistake. Many alcoholics and drug ad
the common addiction to prescribed tranquilizers) resor
numbing relief of chemicals because they do not conside
competent to cope. This invariably has ruinous effects on
and their families. The *yetzer hara* has then achieved its goal of crushing a person by means of the delusion of inferiority and inadequacy.

A particularly ruinous avoidance of coping is *procrastination.* Ramchal, who is very careful with his choice of words, says of procrastination, "There is no danger as great as that of procrastination" (*Mesillas Yesharim, Zerizus*). The reason for this is that procrastination is self-deception. Deciding not to do something is not fooling oneself. The procrastinator who thinks, *I will do it, but just not now,* is deceiving himself. One does not want to do something, but does not want to admit that. Instead, the task is postponed, and, typically, it is never done at all.

Procrastination is a trait that is difficult to overcome. There are suggestions on ways one can overcome procrastination, but of course, the procrastinator never gets around to doing them.

Relationships

The most serious problems in life are those that go unrecognized. The lethality of cancer is that it so often remains silent, and when it does produce symptoms, the disease may be dangerously advanced.

This is also true of low self-esteem. I am a typical case in point. As noted, I was a rabbi for ten years and a practicing psychiatrist for eight years, and I had no idea that my self-image was so distorted.

It stands to reason that unwarranted feelings of unworthiness and inferiority can seriously affect interpersonal relationships. A person who feels undeserving of love may be stymied in marriage. There are cases of young men and women, who, because they felt they were unattractive or undesirable company, tried to behave in a way to impress the partner, but this false front sabotaged the relationship. A man who nurses his low self-esteem by domineering others may be an abuser, with harmful effects on his wife and children. A woman with low self-esteem may accept abuse because she thinks she is inadequate as a wife.

Yoni and Chavi consulted me. They had been married for eight months and felt that their relationship was deteriorating, but had no clue why.

Yoni is a physicist, very bright and extremely knowledgeable. He is an example of "the paradox of self-esteem," meaning that gifted people are apt to have very low self-esteem. Yoni's defensive maneuver was to dazzle people with his brilliance. The technique can be expressed as, "Look at what I know and what I can do, but don't look at me."

Yoni used this technique during their courtship, and Chavi knew that she was marrying a genius. Once they were married, Yoni began to feel very uncomfortable, because the maneuver of "Look at what I know and what I can do, but don't look at me," can work well in short-term contacts, but not in a long-term personal relationship. Yoni was afraid that when Chavi would discover the miserable wretch that he felt himself to be, he would lose her respect and love.

To prevent Chavi from making this discovery, Yoni began to distance himself from her. Chavi misinterpreted his withdrawal as lack of caring. The relationship was headed for the rocks.

I told them what I felt was happening. Yoni joined a therapy group for self-esteem enhancement, and they received couples therapy as well. Their marriage thrived.

In *How to Break an Addictive Relationship,* psychotherapist Dr. Howard M. Halpern describes cases of women who were in abusive relationships and were advised to leave the marriage, but because of their unwarranted low self-esteem they did not think they could manage on their own. Some people, because they feel inadequate, develop a sick dependency on others.

There is also the phenomenon of hero worship. A person who does not feel worthy in his own right may attach himself to a person whom he glorifies, and feeling himself as an appendage to this person, shares in the glory or strength of his hero. This is why adherents to a cult leader cannot recognize the destructive nature of the cult. Their identification with the cult leader soothes the distress of their low self-esteem.

A person with low self-esteem may develop an identity as a victim. He feels sorry for himself. He feels that no one in the world cares about him, and the world is cruel to him. Sometimes, this person may resist any help that is offered him because he needs to feel victimized.

Real vs. Imagined Shortcomings

I cannot emphasize strongly enough that the problematic, pathological low self-esteem is the result of *unwarranted and unjustified* feelings of inadequacy. These are not reality. If a person has actual limitations which are reality, these are not delusional and do not contribute to low self-esteem.

As a child, I loved baseball. I was an avid follower of my home team. I loved to play baseball, but unfortunately I could neither hit nor catch a ball. Needless to say, when the kids chose teams, I was never picked.

I was desperate to play. You may not believe it, but in 1942, you could get ten caramel candies for a penny! I brought candy to school and used them to try to bribe the kids to let me play. They took the candy, but did not pick me for their teams.

About a block away from the school, there was a sporting goods store. Displayed in the window was a Louisville slugger baseball bat with a blue-felt handle—a real treasure. The kids used to press their noses against the store window and gaze at the bat. But they were in dreamland. The bat cost $1.25, and in those days, a family of four could live comfortably on $35 a week. We kids felt that only a billionaire could afford the bat.

I saved my Chanukah *gelt* and bought the bat. When I brought it to school, the kids went berserk. "Look at him! He's got the bat! Hey, kid, can we use the bat?"

I said, "Only if I play."

The kids chose sides, and all the players were picked, except me. The two team captains said to each other, "We've gotta pick him. It's his bat!"

One said, "Okay, you take him."

The other responded, "Why should I take him? I've already got Eddie, and he stinks too."

Their dialogue over who would get stuck with me continued until one captain, with Solomonic wisdom, said, "Okay, I'll take him, but his 'outs' don't count."

They invented a new position, "deep right field," to which no one ever hit a ball. I had my turn at bat, waving the bat three times to strike out. That's how I got to play.

Eventually I got tired of this sham. I let the boys use the bat, and I went to the library to study. I was good at that.

My lack of ability at sports did not contribute whatsoever to my low self-esteem because it was a reality: I could not hit or catch. Low self-esteem results from feelings of inadequacy *that are unwarranted* in reality. It is because they are delusional that they create problems.

If you have a shortcoming that is factual, it is possible to successfully compensate for it, just as a blind person develops exquisite senses of touch and hearing. The fact was that I was inadequate in athletics, so I compensated for it by excelling in academics. But if one's feelings of inadequacy are delusional, there is no way to compensate for a delusion. It is like trying to fill a pitcher that has a hole in the bottom. No matter how many attempts one makes, one cannot fill it.

It has been pointed out that *mussar* repeatedly stresses that we are always in arrears: regardless of how much we do, we have never done enough toward self-improvement. Shouldn't that depress one's self-esteem?

The answer is, "Decidedly not!"

I have pointed out that the danger of low self-esteem is its delusional nature. Shortcomings that exist in reality do not depress self-esteem. Indeed, they stimulate us to growth.

Mussar teaches us that our goal should be to establish closeness to Hashem through Torah. Inasmuch as Torah is infinite, we can never exhaust it. R' Nachum of Chernobyl cited the verse "The Torah of Hashem is whole" (*Psalms* 19:8), and commented, "The Torah is always whole, because no one has ever bitten off a piece of it." The greatest *tzaddikim* felt that they fell short of the goal. But this is a shortcoming that is factual and not delusional; hence it does not depress self-esteem.

One of my methods to alleviate my low self-esteem was to over-achieve. Having emerged to some degree from my negative self-concept, I am now a *high-achiever* instead of an *overachiever.* There is a difference.

Suppose you're driving along at 60 miles per hour, and you come to a very steep hill. You switch into low gear to give you the extra power to climb the hill. Once you're at the top and on level ground, you want to switch back to "drive," but your gear is stuck. You now must drive in low gear, but although it has extra power, the car can't go more than 40 m.p.h. Furthermore, you burn both gas and oil excessively. Low gear was intended for a steep climb, not for cruising.

Overachieving to escape feelings of inadequacy is like driving on flat land in low gear. There is extra power, but it actually slows you down. If you don't have to prove yourself, you can be a high-achiever. You can actually accomplish more with less stress.

I have had teachers who loved to teach. They had much to give to their students and they enjoyed doing it. They were high achievers, not overachievers.

I enjoy writing books, and I do not feel under pressure to do so. I have become a comfortable high-achiever instead of a stress-ridden overachiever.

Protecting the Innocent

Child abuse and molestation are unforgivable crimes. The media has reported many incidents of cover-ups, and those who participate in covering up these heinous crimes are every bit as guilty as the perpetrator.

Victims of abuse and molestation need professional help so that these occurrences should not ruin their lives.

Having said that, it is important to be aware of "psychic reality." A mature adult can distinguish reality from fantasy. A person may have a dream so vivid that he feels it happened in reality and was not just a dream. However, the juvenile mind may not be able to make that distinction. If a child fantasized something, whether in the waking state or in a dream, he may not realize that it was a fantasy. To the child, it is reality. He is certain that what he experienced did actually occur. The child is not concocting stories. He genuinely believes that the incident occurred.

It is not only molestation that must be carefully investigated. Incidents of childhood trauma that adults report should be considered in the light of "psychic reality." Accepting all reports of childhood experiences as factual may cause a serious rift between children and parents. Either dismissing them as fantasy or accepting them as reality might be a mistake.

It is extremely important that what adults report happened to them in childhood be very carefully evaluated. Failure to apprehend a perpetrator is a serious dereliction by the community and its authorities. However, it is also a serious crime to convict an innocent person. Great expertise is required to get at the truth.

So, What Is the Solution?

Let's recapitulate. In addition to negative experiences of the formative years, there is a powerful force that seeks to depress a person and make one feel unworthy and inadequate. This force is the *yetzer hara*, which is universal. Even great Torah scholars and *tzaddikim* are not immune to it.

The feelings of inferiority and unworthiness may be subliminal or may be totally unconscious, yet they exert their effect on a person's emotions, thoughts, and behavior. People may utilize various defensive maneuvers to shield themselves from the discomfort of low self-esteem, and these defenses drain a person's energies and may cause one to become depressed. *Low self-esteem is a delusion*, wrought by the *yetzer hara* that seeks to disable and prevent a person from reaching the potential with which Hashem has endowed one. Unless this force is neutralized, one may live all one's life under this delusionary influence.

Psychotherapy may alleviate those noxious feelings that are the result of early life experiences, but does not and cannot neutralize the *yetzer hara*. As noted, R' Simchah Zissel identified the *yetzer hara* as the culprit, in the verse, "*Dacho dechisani linpol,*" and the obvious solution is also in that verse, "*vaHashem azarani,* Hashem helped me." Other than the help of Hashem, there is no solution to the component of low self-esteem resulting from the *yetzer hara's* crushing force.

However, achieving the help of Hashem in neutralizing the force of the *yetzer hara* is not easily accomplished. It requires much motivation. Unless one understands that surrendering to the *yetzer hara* means living a delusional life with all of its negative consequences, one may not invest the effort to overcome the low self-esteem.

Tefillah, praying to Hashem, to eliminate the force of the *yetzer hara* is indeed important, but is not enough. You must remember that Hashem put the *yetzer hara* within you for a purpose. Yes, He will help you in the battle, but there is much you must do.

One cannot have self-esteem unless one fulfills oneself, becoming that which one was intended to be.

Carnation, a dairy company, advertised that the evaporated milk it sold came from contented cows. Indeed, the standard of excellence for a cow is contentment, because there is nothing else it must do. If all a human being aspires to is to be content — free from pain, stress, and worry — then one has the same objective in life as a cow. Inasmuch as a person is endowed with much more potential than a cow, merely being content does not lead to one's true fulfillment.

Ramchal begins his epochal *Mesillas Yesharim* with the chapter, "Man's Duty in His World." This concept is fundamental to self-fulfillment and self-esteem.

There is an abundance of Torah literature on the struggle with the *yetzer hara*. Most of the *sefarim* deal with subduing the *yetzer hara* and resisting its temptations. While this is certainly of great importance, it is not the whole story, as we shall see in the following chapters.

The Battle with the Yetzer Hara

Most of the material that I am familiar with deals with resisting the *yetzer hara's* temptations, whether it is urging us to violate one of the Torah prohibitions or to refrain from performing a mitzvah. We are told how to defy the *yetzer hara* when it tempts us to desecrate the Shabbos, to eat non-kosher food, to take someone else's belongings, to speak *lashon hara*, to rush through our prayers, to be miserly in giving *tzedakah*. These struggles are not easy, but we have learned how to deal with them.

Certainly, subduing the *yetzer hara's* seduction to committing *aveiros* is of the greatest importance. However, not enough attention has been given to the Talmudic statement, "A person's *yetzer [hara]* renews itself every day ... and seeks to kill him" (*Kiddushin* 30b). It does not say that the *yetzer hara* seeks to cause one to sin, which is indeed implied, but that *it seeks to kill him*. R' Simchah Zissel takes the statement at its face value. By causing a person to feel worthless, to lose one's vital sense of *chashivus*, the *yetzer hara* seeks to crush and destroy a person. And the Talmud states that without Hashem's help, one cannot possibly defeat the *yetzer hara*.

Mesillas Yesharim and other *sifrei mussar* tell us that Hashem had a specific design for creating man. The Baal Shem Tov's interpretation of the Divine statement, "Let us make man" (*Genesis* 1:26), is that Hashem was seeking man's participation in his own creation. Hashem created angels as totally spiritual beings, and He created animals as totally physical beings. Hashem's will was to create a being that is fully physical, like all other animals, but is unique in that he can become spiritual through his own efforts. Indeed, man comes into the world as "a wild mule" (*Job* 11:12). Hashem wishes to give of His infinite goodness to man, but in order that this be the ultimate good, it must be earned. Hashem, therefore, created the *yetzer hara* to deter man from becoming spiritual, and by vanquishing the *yetzer hara*, man merits the reward for becoming spiritual.

The goal of the *yetzer hara* can be summed up in just a few words. *The yetzer hara wishes to prevent man from fulfilling the Divine will to become spiritual.* It wants man to remain "the wild mule" he was at birth. The *yetzer hara* has no problem with allowing a person to become more knowledgeable and intelligent.

The battle with the *yetzer hara* arises when a person wishes to be something more, when one wishes to break loose from simple animalistic self-gratification and achieve a higher level of existence instead of being preoccupied with satisfying one's physical desires.

The chassidic master, R' Simchah Bunim of P'shische, shared R' Simchah Zissel's interpretation of the Talmudic statement.

He wrote, "A person must conceptualize the yetzer hara as an enemy wielding a sword and threatening to behead one."

One chassid asked, "What if one cannot conceptualize that?"

R' Simchah Bunim replied, "That means that the enemy was already successful in beheading him."

In modern times, especially in Israel, we must be on constant alert for terrorists, whose only goal is to destroy us, even at the cost of suicide. Any relaxation of our alertness, any weakening of our defenses is an invitation to the terrorist. R' Simchah Bunim recognized the *yetzer hara* as a terrorist, bent on destroying a person.

The *yetzer hara* must be recognized as a malignant force, as lethal to one's spiritual life as physical malignancies are to one's physical life. It must also be recognized that preventing the lethal effects of this malignancy may require aggressive measures.

We can better understand the Talmudic statement, "*Reshaim* are considered dead even during their lifetime" (*Berachos* 18a). They are physically alive, but it is only their animal component, their self-gratifying component, that is alive. What distinguishes a human being from animals is spirituality, and if a person is absorbed solely in physicality and is devoid of spirituality, his human component is dead. This is the meaning of the Talmud, "A person's *yetzer hara* renews itself every day and seeks to kill him." In other words, it seeks to destroy the human component of one's existence.

The antidote to the destructive force of the *yetzer hara* is *spirituality*, becoming the unique creature that Hashem intended man to be.

Repelling the Yetzer Hara

When the *yetzer hara* urges you to do something forbidden on Shabbos or tempts you to eat something non-kosher, you recognize its attempt, and you use the familiar tools to resist it. However, when you feel unworthy or inadequate, you may not recognize that this, too, is the mark of the *yetzer hara*, and you may succumb to its wiles. Once you begin to feel unworthy, the *yetzer hara* has sunk its claws into you and it is difficult to dislodge it. That is why it is important to repel the *yetzer hara* so that it does not take hold of you. It is very much like the sting of a yellow jacket, whose pain may be difficult to subdue. It is most effective to use an insect repellent, which will prevent the sting from happening. As with any disease, prevention is more effective than treatment.

The greatest military success is often brought about by a pre-emptive strike. The Talmud applies this to the battle with the *yetzer hara*. "A person should always incite the *yetzer tov* against the *yetzer hara*" (*Berachos* 8a). This is far more effective than defending oneself against it, which occurs once the *yetzer hara* has succeeded in getting a foothold. How does one make a preemptive strike? With *simchah*!

R' Levi Yitzchak of Berditchev says that *simchah* is a powerful repellent of the *yetzer hara*. But we cannot rely on the spontaneous *simchah* that is dependent on happy occasions, because these are not constant. R' Nachman of Breslov said, "It is a great mitzvah to *constantly* have *simchah*." All the *sifrei chassidus* and *mussar* stress the importance of *simchah*. We must be able to generate *simchah* at all times.

King David gives us the formula for generating *simchah*. "Serve Hashem with gladness, come before Him with joyous song. Know that Hashem, He is G-d; He made us and we are His, His people and the sheep of His pasture. Enter His gates with thanksgiving ..." (*Psalms* 100:2-4).

And again, "May the heart of those who seek Hashem be glad" (ibid., 105:3). If we seek closeness to Hashem, and realize that we are His chosen people, we will feel *simchah*.

But, how often do we meditate on this and realize our incomparable uniqueness as the children of Hashem? The Talmud says, "Beloved are the people Israel, for they are described as children of the Omnipresent; it is indicative of a greater love that it was made known to them that they are described as children of the Omnipresent ..." (*Ethics of the Fathers* 3:18). We should never forget this.

The *yetzer hara* may remind you of your actions in order to disparage you. Retaining your irrevocable uniqueness can protect you from accepting this disparagement.

The Talmud relates that King Solomon was banished from his throne by the demon, Ashmadai, and cast into a distant part of the land. Solomon walked about, dressed as a homeless beggar, declaring, "I am King Solomon." He was mocked at as deranged (*Gittin* 68b). The Midrash says that whereas he had previously been king of an empire, he was now king only over his walking stick. The commentaries say that Solomon retained his sense of royalty, albeit it was only over his walking stick. Never losing his sense of sovereignty enabled Solomon to regain the throne.

My great-grandmother suffered with Alzheimer's disease. She said, "I don't know who I am and I don't know where I am. But I do know *whose* I am." She was referring to her father, the *tzaddik* Zeide Reb Motele. We should always remember Whose we are. This is something the *yetzer hara* cannot take from us.

The psychiatrist, Viktor Frankl, was imprisoned in the Auschwitz concentration camp. He writes that the Nazis stripped him of everything he owned, even his clothes, but they could not take away his attitude. Even if he were to die, he had the choice of how to face death. Regardless of what the *yetzer hara* tries to do to you, it can never take away your awareness of Whose you are.

How often do we contemplate the awesome infinity of Hashem's majesty? How often do we think of the great privilege we have of relating to Hashem? Especially on Shabbos, when we are the recipients of the precious gift of which Hashem said to Moses, "I have a wonderful gift in My treasure house and Shabbos is its name, and I wish to give it to the Children of Israel; go and inform them" (*Beitzah*

16a). Regardless of the level of spirituality one has during the week, when Shabbos comes, Hashem gives us an additional *neshamah* and a superb *kedushah*. If we are not moved to dance for joy, we are remiss in our appreciation of Shabbos.

If we truly understand our good fortune in being chosen by Hashem to be His people, our attitude would be different. One *tzaddik* said, "When I wake up in the morning and say, '*Modeh ani lefanecha*,' and I realize who is this little '*ani*' and Who is the '*lefanecha*,' I am awestruck and cannot continue. I struggle my way to the *berachos*, and when I say *Shelo asani goy*, and realize that Hashem has chosen me as a Jew, my spirits soar, and I can continue davening with courage and *simchah*.

The importance of *simchah* in *Yiddishkeit* can be gleaned from the statement in *Deuteronomy* (28:47), where, after describing the terrible consequences that will befall Israel if it does not observe the Torah, the verse states this would be "because you did not serve Hashem, your G-d, amid gladness and goodness of heart." If *simchah* is only an emotion that results from pleasant occasions, how could the Torah hold us responsible for failure to have *simchah*? Obviously, we are capable of generating *simchah* at any time and we are derelict if we do not do so.

A firm *emunah* (faith) in Hashem will enable us to appreciate our good fortune in being the chosen children of Hashem. Perhaps this is what is meant by the Talmudic statement that the prophet Habakkuk encapsulated the entire Torah in the single principle, "The righteous person shall live through his *emunah*" (*Habakkuk* 2:4).

Firm *emunah* is much more than a *frumkeit* issue. *Emunah* will enable a person to generate *simchah*, which in turn will enable one to repel the destructive influence of the *yetzer hara*. *Emunah* is thus necessary for life, and in this light, we can understand Habakkuk's statement, "The righteous person shall live through his *emunah*."

How can one attain firm *emunah*? Of course, studying the great works of chassidus and *mussar* is essential, but nothing is as effective in developing and strengthening *emunah* as seeing how our great *tzaddikim* lived. The Talmud says that the narrative regarding Eliezer, the servant of Abraham, is dearer to Hashem than the scholarly works of the Sages (*Bereishis Rabbah* 60:11). This is because every move that the patriarch made was a concrete expression of Hashem's will.

We are fortunate in having accounts of how our *tzaddikim* conducted their lives. They were able to generate *simchah* regardless of the circumstances they experienced.

In our own times, there was a *tzaddik* who was an acknowledged Torah scholar, R' Shlomo Zalman Auerbach (1910-1995). It is of interest that when he died and his obituary was published, the newspaper editors searched for an appropriate photo of him. Every photo of R' Shlomo Zalman showed him smiling, and the editors thought it inconsistent to have a smiling face in a black frame of mourning.

R' Shlomo Zalman's constant *simchah* was due to his absolute adherence to Torah. When his wife died, R' Shlomo Zalman said, "It is the practice to ask *mechilah* (forgiveness) at a funeral. But we lived our life according to Torah, and there is nothing for which I should ask *mechilah*." Think of it! To live in a close relationship with another person for more than sixty years, and to be secure in the knowledge that one never offended the other!

We can better understand how R' Shlomo Zalman achieved this from the following anecdote. He was escorted to his home by several of his students, and before he entered his house, he brushed off his jacket and straightened his hat. He explained to his students, "The Talmud says that when a man and wife live together harmoniously, the *Shechinah* (Divine Presence) dwells with them. I am about to enter my home, where the *Shechinah* resides, and I must make my appearance decent in respect of the *Shechinah*."

There are many other *tzaddikim* of our own generation whose lives are a testimony to their sincere *emunah* in Hashem. They had a true *simchas hachaim*, a happiness of life, which did not allow the *yetzer hara* to obtain a foothold in their lives.

Living a life of sincere *emunah* generates *simchah* that repels the *yetzer hara* and does not permit it to exert its nefarious tactics to crush a person by undermining one's self-esteem.

The Simchah Soliloquy of R' Leib, Son of Sarah (1730-1781)

We can all learn about true happiness from this soliloquy. As a preface to this ode to *simchah*, here is the background of its author.

In the Russia and Poland of yesteryear, Jews were denied the privilege of living in the larger cities, and there were many restrictions on what they could do to earn their livelihood. Consequently, many Jews operated inns at the side of the roads. Since they lived so far from town, they could not send their children to *cheder*, and therefore many innkeepers hired a live-in tutor, a *melamed*, for their children.

Joseph was an elderly widower who was a *melamed* at an inn. One day, the local *poritz* (feudal lord) stopped at the inn, and when he saw the innkeeper's charming daughter, he said, "I'm going to take that young woman as my wife. I will return in a few days with my priest to conduct the marriage." The *poritz* had absolute authority and control in his fiefdom, and could imprison or execute anyone at his whim. The innkeeper and his daughter were horrified.

The young woman, Sarah, said, "I will never let that fiend touch me. I know what I can do. I will marry someone else, and the priest will not allow him to take a married woman."

The innkeeper said, "But there is no one here who is appropriate for you to marry."

Sarah said, "I will marry Joseph, and the *poritz* will not be able to touch me."

When Joseph heard her plan, he protested, "My child, what are you saying? You are young and I am a very old man."

But Sarah was adamant, "You, Joseph, are the only one who can save me."

They gathered a *minyan*, and Sarah married Joseph that very day. Indeed, the *poritz's* plan was stymied, as the priest would not allow him to marry a woman who was already married.

Later that year, Sarah bore Joseph a son, whom they named Aryeh Leib. Joseph did not live to see Aryeh Leib's bar mitzvah. Before his death, he told Aryeh Leib that he should never forget his mother's *mesiras nefesh* (self-sacrifice).

Aryeh Leib later became a follower of the Baal Shem Tov; he is known in chassidic lore as "R' Leib Sarah's (Sarah's Reb Leib)." There are many legends about R' Leib Sarah's. He took upon himself the mission of liberating Jews from the dungeons in which the feudal lords had imprisoned them.

He often traveled from village to village on foot. One spring day, as he made his way along the paths and fields, he was overcome with spiritual rapture at the beauty of nature, and was inspired to author this amazing prose poem.

> *Ribbono shel Olam (Master of the Universe)! How can I ever praise and thank You for all the good and kindness, the glory and the beauty that You have shown me? After all the prayers of David son of Yishai have been exhausted, who am I and what am I to say to You "Bless Hashem, O my soul. Hashem my G-d, You are very great."" But this I will say to you, my Father in Heaven, Leib, the son of Sarah, is fortunate, very fortunate. He has so much; he is very strong. Who among the most wealthy can compare himself to me? Yes, they have silver, gold, homes, and estates, but all these have limits, but to Leib, the son of Sarah, You have given an inheritance that has no limits. You have put everything at his feet, mountains, valleys, fields, and forests. All the land that he can see is his. Who is really wealthy? If a person has a home and estate surrounded by a fence; and if he is very wealthy he also has a coach and a pair or two pairs of horses. If he is still wealthier, he has a number of servants. Leib, the son of Sarah, has seen many wealthy people, but he has never seen a wealthy person who is happy. Leib has looked into this and he found that there is no true pleasure in wealth. The more one possesses, the greater are one's worries. As one's pleasure increases, so does the worry and anguish that all this "good" may be lost. All the days of a wealthy man are bad, because he lives in fear, fearful that his wealth will not endure. He fears that someone*

else may be wealthier than he, he is in fear of thieves or that some catastrophe will impoverish him. This fear robs the wealthy person of peace of mind. Since he has no peace of mind, he cannot be happy. He has no security, no hour of nachas. Even at night, his heart is not at rest. Leib has seen many wealthy people in his day, but none who ever enjoyed pleasant, sweet sleep. The wealthy man cannot sleep even a bit without guards at his gate and vicious dogs at his fence. The wealthy constantly wallow in gold dust, but who can brush off this dust from their eyes so that they could see the true gold that covers Your beautiful world? Ribbono shel Olam! The wealthy have eyes but do not see that Your world is majestic, beautiful, and radiant. It is a painful place for them.

But I, Leib, the son of Sarah, am happy, because I lack for nothing, my Heavenly Father. I lack nothing. You have blessed me, Father, so that the whole world is my home. My feet carry me to all four corners of the earth to save Jewish lives. I gather sparks, merciful Father, for there are sparks everywhere. Wherever I go, I find the sparks, and wherever I go, Jews come along with me. Jews greet me, whether in the fields or in the woods, I meet Jews, and when I come to the outskirts of a town, they come out to greet me and say "Shalom Aleichem, Reb Yehudi."

Leib, the son of Sarah, is a king, a king without an army, without fortresses, without ministers and servants. He is a king who wanders along the paths, but a king nevertheless. His bundle on his shoulder cannot be equaled by the gold of the great kings. It is not a bundle, but a collection of hearts. It contains all the good hearts of the Jews, all the feelings of mercy between a Jew and his fellow. It contains all the mitzvos and good deeds that Jews fulfill with their money, whether one does much or little. One perutah (small coin) for tzedakah is as good as one hundred. Whether one is rich or poor, no one turns down Leib, the son of Sarah. Everyone donates with good will and generously. They pour money into my treasury. Leib, the son of Sarah, is very wealthy. Not only does he always have a coin in his purse, but he sees Your world, Ribbono shel Olam, in its splendor and in its majestic charm. How fortunate is Leib, the son of Sarah. It is good with Leib, very good. Leib is full of joy. I wish, Ribbono shel Olam, that Leib could be as happy every day, every time, and every hour, as he is now, an endless happiness so that he could bring happiness to every Jewish heart.

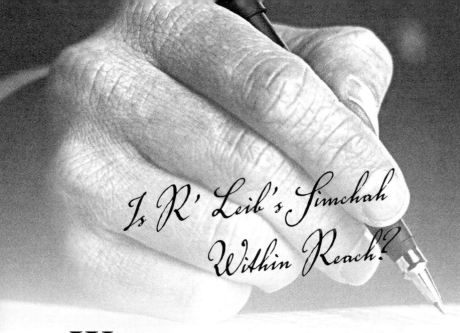

Is R' Leib's Simchah Within Reach?

We read stories about our *gedolim*, and we may say, "They were indeed very great, with enormous spirituality, but we are unable to aspire to that." That is a mistake. Many of our *gedolim* struggled to become who they were. R' Hutner responded to a young man who asked about this issue, "We don't know how many battles the Chofetz Chaim fought and how many spiritual hardships he had to overcome until he achieved his greatness in Torah and *middos*."

Can we achieve the *simchah* of R' Leib Sarah's? Perhaps, but to do so we must divest ourselves of the limited concept of *simchah* that we have.

A peasant came to the big city, and walking past a men's clothing store, he saw a handsome suit displayed. He entered the shop and asked the salesman for a suit. The salesman estimated his size and gave him a suit to try on in the dressing room. The peasant emerged from the dressing room, seething with anger at the salesman for giving him a suit that doesn't fit him at all.

The salesman saw that the peasant had put the suit on over his farmer's clothes and said, "My friend, you have to take off your old clothes. No suit will fit properly if you wear it on top of your old clothes."

We might wonder why we have difficulty achieving an enduring *simchah*. It is because we are trying to put it on top of our former concept of *simchah*. Most people think of *simchah* as the thrilling feeling one has on a happy occasion, such as a wedding, bar mitzvah, Simchas Torah, Purim, or other event when we feel joyous, and that stimulates us to sing and dance. But this is a very narrow definition of *simchah*. As long as we are looking for this exotic experience, we will not find the *simchah* of R' Leib Sarah's.

The clearest definition of a concept is often derived by contrasting it with its opposite. Thus, we can better understand heat as the opposite of cold, and vice versa. We may better understand *simchah* by contrasting it with its opposite. The opposite of *simchah* is despair.

There were some stories that my father repeated a number of times. I am certain that this was because he wished to impress upon us the importance of the message conveyed by the story. One such story is the following parable:

A man was sentenced to 25 years of hard labor. His wrists were shackled to the handle of a huge wheel that was set in the wall. All his waking hours, he had to turn this massive wheel. He would often wonder what it was that he was doing. Perhaps he was grinding grain into flour or bringing up well water to irrigate fields.

After the long sentence was completed and the shackles were removed, he hurried to the other side of the wall to see what he had been accomplishing. Upon seeing that the wheel was not attached to anything, he collapsed. Twenty-five years of backbreaking work — all for nothing! He was able to survive 25 years of bone-crushing labor, but the feeling that it had been futile, all for naught, was more than he could bear. He simply gave up and died of despair.

One can endure hard work under difficult circumstances due to the satisfaction of accomplishing something worthwhile. When this man discovered that all his work was for naught he fell apart.

The Maggid of Mezeritch said that we should learn three things from babies.

> 1. Babies are always happy.

> 2. When a baby wants something, it cries. By this the Maggid meant that when we pray to Hashem for our wants and needs, we should do so with such intensity that it brings us to tears.

➤ 3. Babies are never idle. They are always doing something.

Observe toddlers. They are crawling on all fours looking everywhere. They crawl under things and try to crawl over things that stand in their way. Toddlers are curious. There is so much in the world that is new to them, and they are constantly investigating their world. Toddlers do not rest before they are so exhausted that they fall asleep, but as long as they are awake, they are on the go.

How different from adults, who look for opportunities to relax. This is because we have lost our curiosity. We are familiar with our world, that is, with that part of the world that is in our immediate surroundings. Because we have lost our curiosity, we are not motivated to activity, and we look forward to relaxing.

Yes, the Maggid is right. Toddlers are always happy because they are always active, trying to learn more about the world. We adults have confined ourselves to a narrow space and have resigned ourselves to live within it.

But the world is full of so many exciting things! If we can afford to travel, we can visit places of exquisite, breathtaking beauty. If we cannot afford to travel, we can see the miracles of Hashem's creations in photographs or on videos. Places of historic significance are fascinating, and if we cannot visit them we can read about them and discover history. Art, music, and literature abound in concepts we can learn. The world of science is virtually infinite, full of data that attest to Hashem's great wisdom in creation. And of course, there is the inexhaustible wisdom of the Torah. One can study the Torah for decades and there is always so much more one could learn. But unfortunately, we are not curious. We are satisfied with plugging along in our everyday lives, which so often becomes boring, and boredom does not permit happiness.

Toddlers are always happy because they are not bored. Everything in their world is so fresh and so exciting that they may howl with glee at every new discovery, but they are constantly stretching the boundaries, looking for more things in the world that they may find interesting and that fill them with joy.

R' Samson Raphael Hirsch made an important observation. R' Hirsch, among others, contends that when two Hebrew words are similar, their meanings are somehow related. The words *samei'ach* (happiness) and *tzomei'ach* (growth) are almost identical. This means that *simchah* requires growth. There is a seed of *simchah* within every person that can be developed into happiness, but like a delicate plant, it must be cared for and given adequate water and nutrition. Only then can it sprout.

The problem is that in modern times we are reluctant to nurture this seed to make it grow. Our technology has eliminated so much of the work to achieve a final product. We want everything to be instant and ready made. To make gefilte fish, my mother would buy fresh fish, grind it, chop it, season it, and cook it. To make dinner, she would eviscerate a chicken, soak it, and salt it before cooking it. Each step was part of a laborious process. Today, our food — and much else — is "ready for the pot." This has so influenced our thinking that we want happiness, too, to be "ready for the pot," achievable without any effort on our part. Millions of people have become dependent on prescription tranquilizers in the desire to get a "quick fix" of happiness. Drugs may numb their minds so that they don't feel their unhappiness so acutely, but they are far, far from happy.

Our technology has given us many inventions that give us instant results: fax machines, jet planes, email. We do not have the patience that growth requires. We think that there must be some gadget or method that will give us happiness.

We should accept the reality that our technology cannot give us happiness, nor can we get it from objects in our environment. All the claims that "I would be happy if only ..." are deceptive. You are free to fool yourself, but the only true happiness is reached by nurturing the seed within us. We must accept that we can find true happiness only if we invest the time and effort necessary for the seed of happiness to sprout. We should rid ourselves of the term "pursuit of happiness," as if it can be reached and grasped, and think of "development of happiness" instead, because it is an ongoing process without a definite end zone.

True, it takes effort and expenditure of energy to investigate our world and learn more about it. But this is a small price to pay for the happiness we may get from growing (*tzomei'ach*) in knowledge.

We believe that our purpose in life is to have a close relationship with Hashem, and the means to accomplish this is the observance of Torah. Every time one does a mitzvah, one draws closer to Hashem. Every mitzvah is thus a true achievement, and one should, therefore, feel *simchah* in doing a mitzvah.

There are stories of how our *gedolim* rejoiced when performing a mitzvah. It is related that on the night after the last day of Pesach, R' Levi Yitzchak of Berditchev sat at the window, looking for the first signs of dawn. The dawn would enable him to put on his *tefillin*, which he had been unable to do for the eight days of the festival. He longed for the joy of performing that mitzvah again after a full week.

I had a *melamed* who was bothered by a problem in the Talmud that he could not resolve. When he finally found a *sefer* that discussed this problem and explained it, he kissed the *sefer* and danced with it in pure happiness that the issue had been resolved.

We should have firm *emunah* that we were chosen to do the will of Hashem, and that this is the greatest privilege a person could have. We should, therefore, be thrilled when we have the opportunity to do a mitzvah, whether it is to give *tzedakah*, recite the *bentching* after meals, observe Shabbos, eat in the *succah*, or any other of the many mitzvos. True, we feel joy at celebrating a bar mitzvah or a wedding, but as time goes on, these memories fade. But every mitzvah one does is permanent, and one should feel the privilege and happiness of having done a mitzvah even after ten or twenty years.

Conflicting feelings can coexist. If a person who was overjoyed when he won millions of dollars later developed a severe headache, he would indeed be bothered by the pain, but that would not diminish his joy of winning the lottery. Similarly, the difficulties one experiences in life should not erase the *simchah* of having done a mitzvah. The *simchah* and the pain can coexist.

Just as the performance of a mitzvah is a great merit, so is the preparation for doing the mitzvah a great merit. One should feel *simchah* in building the *succah*, even though the actual mitzvah will be done later. One should feel *simchah* in preparing for Shabbos.

Inasmuch as one cannot perform the mitzvos properly unless one is in optimal health, we can consider maintaining our health as preparation for doing mitzvos. We need proper nutrition to have the ability to do mitzvos. Thus, eating can be seen as a preparation for doing mitzvos, and in this way, eating is not just satisfying one's hunger, but can also be a mitzvah. If one eats with the intention that one will have the ability to do mitzvos, one may justifiably feel *simchah* when eating. In this way, we can convert much of our daily life into an achievement of doing mitzvos and becoming closer to Hashem. Our entire day can become a *simchah shel mitzvah*, and we can feel this *simchah* even in the presence of circumstances that may cause us to feel unhappy.

The *yetzer hara* is very wily. It deceives us and makes us think that satisfying our desires will make us happy; all too often, we allow ourselves to be deceived.

In our *tefillos* on the festivals, we thank Hashem for giving us "*moadim l'simchah.*" The correct translation of this is not "festivals *of* joy," but rather "festivals *for* joy." Properly observed, the festivals should be a source of *simchah* for all year round.

Let us begin with Shabbos. As noted, Hashem told Moshe Rabbeinu, "I have a special gift in My treasury that I wish to give to Israel. Its name is Shabbos." While we observe Shabbos by refraining from doing forbidden acts, we often fail to derive the *simchah* that Shabbos can give us. There is a charming story regarding the *simchah* of Shabbos.

> One Motza'ei Shabbos, the Baal Shem Tov took several of his disciples and traveled to the town of Apta, where he sent for Shabsi, the bookbinder. "Tell me, Shabsi," the Baal Shem Tov said, "What did you do this past Friday night?"

Shabsi said, "I had no money to buy provisions for Shabbos, not even challah or candles. In the afternoon, I told my wife that I did not want her to ask for help from the neighbors. I said that if it pleases Hashem that we have a barren Shabbos, I accept the decree. I then left for the beis midrash.

"In cleaning the house for Shabbos, my wife found a pearl that had fallen off her wedding headpiece. She sold the pearl and bought everything in honor of Shabbos. When I returned home and found the table set and the candles lit, I was upset because I thought my wife had asked for help from the neighbors. When my wife told me that she had found the pearl, I was so elated that Hashem had provided us with everything we needed for a great Shabbos that my wife and I danced around the Shabbos table."

The Baal Shem Tov said, "I want you to know, Shabsi, that when you danced around the Shabbos table, the heavenly angels danced along with you. Your rejoicing over Shabbos is a great mitzvah, and whatever you wish for now will be granted."

Shabsi said, "We have no children, and my only wish is to have a child."

The Baal Shem Tov said, "You will have a son this year, and you should give him my name, Yisrael."

This child became the great chassidic master, the Maggid of Kozhnitz.

How often do we dance around the Shabbos table? We live in a frenetic world, where we are under constant stress and pressure. We are so busy with life that we don't take out the time to think of the purpose of life. On Shabbos, we are free of the distractions of the workweek, and we should be able to reflect on the purpose of our lives.

Earlier, I noted that there is *simchah* in self-fulfillment. During the hectic workweek, we do not have the time to think about self-fulfillment and how we can achieve this. By giving us the time to daven in a more meaningful way, to study Torah, and to think about self-fulfillment, Shabbos can enable us to have true *simchah*.

Generic Spirituality and Spirituality Deficiency Syndrome

As noted, Hashem intended all humans to be different than animals. If a person functions only at an animal level, one is incomplete, and a deficient person cannot have self-esteem. Intelligence has often been cited as the unique distinguishing feature separating humans from animals. According to this, a multiple-degreed person with the most advanced intellect would then be the most perfect human being. Obviously, this is not so. A highly educated person can also be vulgar, selfish, cruel, and immoral — hardly attributes one would consider comprising an ideal human being. The "something else" that gives human beings their uniqueness is more than just intellect. I have listed many of these traits in "To My Great-Grandson," beginning on page 200.

The sum total of all the traits that are unique to humans is what we may refer to as the human "spirit." As noted, all these features are uniquely human *abilities.* For example, a person may or may not reflect on the purpose of his existence, but every human being has the *ability* to do so. If one exercises and implements these elements of the spirit, then one is being *spiritual.* Spirituality can, therefore, be thought of as *being the best human being one can be.*

Whereas the body is tangible, the spirit is an abstract concept. The body makes its needs known very dramatically and emphatically through the feelings of hunger, thirst, anger, pain, and weariness, among others. We are closely familiar with the body, and we do not have to ponder whether or not the body exists in reality. The spirit, although very real, is intangible. We cannot see or touch it, and it does not make its needs known as emphatically as the body.

The body can be tyrannical. It makes loud demands, and is easily habituated. Give the body cigarettes for a period of time, and if then deprived of nicotine will produce symptoms that are likely to drive one back to smoking. The body may become habituated to alcohol, drugs, or to anything that gives it pleasure.

Animals are slaves to the body; they cannot make choices that defy the body's demands. Human beings that comply primarily with the demands of the body are similarly slaves to it. Albert Einstein said, "The true value of a human being is determined primarily by the measure and the sense in which he has attained to liberation from the self." He was referring to the common concept of the self as the body. Freeing oneself from the tyranny of the body allows the true self, the spirit, to emerge. This, Einstein said, is the true value of a human being.

I believe that just as the lack of essential bodily nutrients results in a physical deficiency, failure to provide the spirit with its essential nutrients results in a "spirituality deficiency syndrome" (SDS). The primary symptom of SDS is *chronic discontent*. This discontent is not the same as clinical depression, and will not be relieved by antidepressant medication, just as an iron-deficiency syndrome will not be cured by antibiotics. Deficiency conditions respond only to administration of the specific nutrient that is lacking. The discontent of SDS can be relieved only by providing the spirit with its essential nutrients, which consists of implementing the uniquely human features that comprise the spirit.

Unfortunately, SDS is often not recognized, and many people are unaware of the real cause for their discontent. It is only natural to seek relief from discomfort, and some people may find short-lived relief in the tranquilizing effects of alcohol or drugs. However, when the effects wear off, the person may turn to more alcohol for relief. It is characteristic for the body to develop *tolerance*, which means that eventually, ever-increasing amounts of alcohol are needed to provide relief, leading to alcohol dependency. This holds true for the relief provided by mood-altering drugs, compulsive gambling, compulsive shopping, compulsive eating, etc. Many addictions develop in an attempt to relieve the discontent of SDS through an escapist technique. This is why spirituality is an essential component of recovery from addiction. It eliminates the haunting, nagging discontent.

Being unaware of the real reason for their discontent, people are likely to attribute it to what *they think* may be the cause. This, together with the recourse to escapist techniques, precludes a person's identifying a deficiency of spirituality as the cause. A human being who is devoid of spirituality is lacking in basic fulfillment and cannot have self-esteem.

Jewish Spirituality

All human beings are obligated to observe the seven Noahide mitzvos. These are:

1. Do not deny G-d.

2. Do not blaspheme G-d.

3. Do not murder.

4. Do not engage in forbidden relationships.

5. Do not steal.

6. Do not eat the flesh of a living animal.

7. Establish courts/legal system to ensure law and obedience.

The Jews were ordered to observe <u>613</u> mitzvos, comprised of 248 positive commandments and 365 prohibitions. Jews are thus held to a higher standard of behavior. The Torah is very clear about the uniqueness of the Jewish people. "For you are a holy people to Hashem, your G-d; Hashem, your G-d, has chosen you to be for Him a treasured people above all the peoples that are on the face of the earth" (*Deuteronomy* 7:6). The level of spirituality required of a Jew is beyond the generic spirituality.

It follows that self-fulfillment of the Jew, which is essential for self-esteem, is more demanding. Also, the crushing force of the *yetzer hara*, which seeks to deter a person from fulfilling one's mission in the world, is greater and more complex.

R' Simchah Zissel's interpretation of *dacho dechisani linpol*, mentioned earlier, is of enormous importance. It draws attention to the powerful force of the *yetzer hara*, and that the only way to resist its destructive force is *vaHashem azarani*, with the help of Hashem. This means not only by *tefillah* but by living in a way that brings one close to Hashem, being a "Jew in essence" and observing the mitzvos. It is important to note that although observance of mitzvos is paramount, *Nesivos Shalom* refers to this as "a Jew in conduct," which is not yet "a Jew in essence."

The concept of the *yetzer hara* and its influence on our behavior is abstract. I've been fortunate in working with alcoholics in recovery to see its function in concrete.

As is well known, Alcoholics Anonymous refers to alcohol as being "cunning, baffling, and powerful." This is an accurate description of the *yetzer hara*. We may naively think we can outsmart it. The alcoholic found that as wise, shrewd, and determined he thought himself to be, alcohol outsmarted him. He finally came to the realization that "only a Power greater than myself" could help him. Everything that is true of alcohol for the alcoholic is true of our battles with the *yetzer hara*.

The Torah relates that the patriarch, Jacob, was attacked by Esau's guardian angel (*Genesis* 32:25). The Midrash gives two versions. One is that the angel appeared like a hostile enemy, and the other is that he appeared like a *talmid chacham*. The *yetzer hara* may masquerade as a *talmid chacham*, as if it is supportive of one's *avodas Hashem*. This is what is meant by "cunning and baffling."

Do not lose sight of the fact that the goal of the *yetzer hara* is to crush you. It may do so by telling you how unworthy you are, reminding you of the *aveiros* you committed or your laxity in Torah and mitzvos. If you get into a discussion or argument with the *yetzer hara* and become defensive, it will defeat you. The proper response is, "Yes, I have committed sins, but that was in the past. I am now dedicated to *teshuvah*, which will erase those sins and bring me closer to Hashem."

As was noted earlier, the *yetzer hara* may try to convince you that it is really the *yetzer tov* and it will preach *mussar* to you. It will tell you that you are, in fact, degraded, and that your *teshuvah* was not genuine. It will cite *sifrei mussar* that say that true *teshuvah* requires much fasting and mortification of the flesh. Do not allow yourself to be deceived. It is really the *yetzer hara* that seeks to depress you and make you feel unworthy.

True *teshuvah* consists of sincere regret for having done wrong, and a sincere commitment to absolutely avoid repetition of the sin. The extreme self-flagellation practiced in the past is not meant for our generation.

A man consulted the tzaddik, R' Michel of Zlotchow, asking what he must do to atone for having inadvertently violated Shabbos. He worked as a porter, and usually came home early on Friday. One Friday, the roads were muddy due to heavy rain, and by the time he came home it was after sunset. R' Michel explained to him the gravity of a Shabbos violation and prescribed the number of days he must fast.

The man consulted the Baal Shem Tov, who told him that the fasting was not necessary, and that he should donate candles to the shul instead. He was overjoyed with this lenient penance and donated the candles.

In those days, candles were made of tallow. A dog picked up the scent of the candles, went into the shul, and ate them. The man replaced the candles, but whenever they were lit, they were promptly extinguished. The man complained to the Baal Shem Tov that Hashem had obviously not accepted his teshuvah.

The Baal Shem Tov understood that this was due to the intervention of R' Michel, and sent a message inviting him to Medzhiboz for Shabbos. R' Michel set out in more than ample time to reach Medzhiboz before Friday noon, but a series of mishaps plagued the trip. An axle of the wagon broke and had to be repaired, then the horse died and had to be replaced, then the wagon fell into a ditch. As a result, R' Michel reached Medzhiboz shortly before sunset.

When he came to the Baal Shem Tov's home, he saw that the Baal Shem Tov was reciting Kiddush. Assuming that it was already Shabbos and that he had traveled by horse and wagon on Shabbos, he fainted.

The Baal Shem Tov revived him and told him that it was not yet Shabbos, but that he had ushered in Shabbos before sunset. Hence, R' Michel had not traveled on Shabbos.

"But tell me," the Baal Shem Tov said, "what did it feel like when you thought that you had traveled on Shabbos? You were overcome with such great fear that you fainted. Do you understand now what a Jew feels like when he realizes that he has inadvertently violated Shabbos? That feeling is true repentance, and there is no need to engage in fasting for forgiveness."

We do fast on Yom Kippur because the Torah commands us to do so, but it is not as a penance for sin; rather, forgiveness is gained by heartfelt remorse.

Further proof that *teshuvah* does not require self-mortification is the halachah in the Talmud that if a person who was known to be a *rasha*, a profligate sinner, proposed marriage to a woman by saying, "I am giving you this wedding item so that you should become my wife, contingent on my being a *tzaddik*," the marriage must be considered valid even though he was the extreme opposite of a *tzaddik*. Why? Because he may have made a mental commitment to do *teshuvah* (*Kiddushin* 49b). It is obvious that a sincere commitment to do *teshuvah* can convert a *rasha* to a *tzaddik*.

Although reflecting on one's sins may be depressing, this emotion should be only superficial. We should rejoice with *teshuvah*.

The Baal Shem Tov visited a village whose residents complained that their chazzan would chant the Vidui (Confession) using a cheerful melody. The Baal Shem Tov

asked the chazzan to explain this rather strange behavior,
and the chazzan said, "If I were the janitor in the king's
palace, and was cleaning the palace to make it more
comfortable for the king, wouldn't I be happy? I have a
Divine neshamah, and when I cleanse myself of my sins, I
am making myself a more decent place for the neshamah to
reside. Isn't that a reason for me to be happy and sing?"

The Baal Shem Tov praised the chazzan highly.

Perhaps this is the reason why we sing Ashamnu with an
upbeat melody.

Yet sincere *teshuvah* should move a person to tears. This is not incompatible with joy, as King David says, "Serve Hashem with awe, that you may rejoice with trembling" (*Psalms* 2:11).

So, do not be taken in by the *yetzer hara's* wiles. It is always necessary that we improve our spiritual status by doing *teshuvah* and by increasing our devotion to Torah and mitzvos, but everything we do should be with *simchah*.

The Most Potent Rebuttal

The Talmud quotes Hashem as saying, "I have created the *yetzer hara*, and I have created Torah as its antidote. If you will observe the Torah, you will not fall into its hands" (*Kiddushin* 30b). If the *yetzer hara* tries to depress you and make you feel unworthy, you can disarm it by doing mitzvos.

> *R' Dovid of Lelov used to travel among the villages to meet Jews. He would say, "They are my brothers. I want to meet my brothers." One time, he was about to go into a house when his chassidim said, "Rebbe, don't go into that house. That man is a rasha."*
>
> *R' Dovid said, "How can you say he is a rasha? Look! He has a mezuzah on his door."*

The fulfillment of even the single mitzvah of *mezuzah* took the man out of the category of *rasha*. So, if the *yetzer hara* tries to make you feel unworthy, say to it, "I am very worthy! I do mitzvos!"

Mitzvos are to the *yetzer hara* what antibiotics are to bacteria. However, one need not have *kavannah* for the antibiotic to work. The potency of mitzvos, however, is greatly increased with proper *kavannah*. When you do a mitzvah, whether it is giving *tzedakah*, reciting the *bentching* after a meal, or any other mitzvah, think, *I am doing the mitzvah that Hashem commanded, and Hashem promised that mitzvos will protect me from the destructive force of the yetzer hara.*

The Talmud says that the *yetzer hara* renews itself every day. If it failed to depress you today, it will try again tomorrow, using different tactics. You can always rebut the *yetzer hara* by doing mitzvos.

We don't make optimal use of this powerful weapon Hashem has given us. If we daven by rote, without thinking about the meaning of the words and without feeling grateful because we have the privilege of communicating with Hashem, we reduce the potency of *tefillah*. With proper *kavannah*, we can vanquish the *yetzer hara*.

The above statement, "I have created the *yetzer hara*, and I have created Torah as its antidote," needs a bit of clarification. If a person swallows poison and is given an effective antidote, the latter will work regardless of the person's attitude. Torah is different. Although learning Torah is the greatest of all mitzvos, the Talmud says, "If a person is meritorious, Torah becomes an elixir of life. If one is not meritorious, Torah becomes a lethal poison" (*Yoma* 72b). Rashi explains that one must learn Torah with the attitude that it is a mitzvah; the *sefarim* add that one should pray that the Torah one is learning should repel and vanquish the *yetzer hara*. Hashem's promise that Torah is an antidote against the *yetzer hara* will be fulfilled.

Kedoshim Tihiyu
(You Will Be Holy)

Do not let the *yetzer hara* degrade you! You are a dear child of Hashem, now and forever.

In *Parashas Kedoshim*, we read:

> You shall be holy, for holy am I, Hashem, your G-d. Every man: Your father and your mother shall you revere and My Sabbaths shall you observe — I am Hashem, your G-d. Do not turn to the idols ... I am Hashem, your G-d (*Leviticus* 19:2-4).

The commentaries note that these three verses could have been combined. The reason each verse is stated separately and each ends with the words, "I am Hashem, your G-d," is to tell us that regardless of what stage of spirituality we are in, we always have a relationship with Hashem. Thus, whether you are holy and of lofty spirituality or whether you simply observe mitzvos such as honoring your parents and observing Shabbos, and even if all you do is reject idolatry, Hashem is always with you.

Vayikra Rabbah 24:9 comments on the words, "You shall be holy, for holy am I, Hashem your G-d," saying "*Yachal kamoni*, you might think you can be as holy as I am; therefore, I tell you, My holiness is superior to yours." The commentaries ask, "What does *yachal kamoni* mean? How could any mortal even dare think that one can be as holy as Hashem?" They answer that inasmuch as our *neshamah* is part of Hashem, one might think one can equal Hashem's holiness. So, if the *yetzer hara* tries to degrade you, remember that you have holiness that is surpassed only by that of Hashem.

When a person commits a sin, one stains only the outer garments of the *neshamah*, which remains forever pure and holy. The proper translation of *kedoshim tihiyu* is not the commandment, "You *shall* be holy"; rather, it is a statement of fact, "You *will* be holy."

The Torah forbids certain actions because they are not becoming of a holy person. If we err, we can correct our behavior and thereby return to our proper level of holiness.

Feelings Are Neutral

The *yetzer hara* may resort to a clever technique to degrade a person and make one feel unworthy. It states that one is a low-grade person for harboring disgusting feelings.

We should realize that *good* and *bad* are judgments that can be made only about actions, not about feelings. We live in a physical body, and we have all the animalistic traits that are characteristic of other living things. Our mission is to refine ourselves, to become spiritual, which means to elevate ourselves above our animalistic nature. We do this by controlling our behavior, so that we are not controlled by these animalistic drives.

We are responsible for our actions, but we cannot be held responsible for feelings that are inherent in our physical body. But the *yetzer hara* will take advantage of these feelings and tell us how debased we are for having "unacceptable" feelings.

Feelings are neither good nor bad. They are just there. For example, hunger is a natural feeling, and one cannot be faulted for feeling hungry. There are, however, several places where the Torah considers feelings to be improper, and we must understand these.

The Torah tells us, "*Lo sachmod*, You shall not covet your fellow's house, his wife ... nor anything that belongs to your fellow" (*Exodus* 20:14). Ibn Ezra asks, "How can one be ordered not to covet something? Desire is a natural feeling that is not subject to voluntary control."

Ibn Ezra answers that a person will not have a desire for something that is unrealistic and not obtainable. A peasant will not have a desire to marry a princess. I believe that the greediest person in the world, who yearns for the treasures displayed in shop windows or on wealthy individuals, will not covet the gold and diamonds that exist in abundance on a distant star, because they are absolutely inaccessible.

Therefore, Ibn Ezra says, if a person will sincerely commit to observing the other commandments, "You shall not steal, you shall not murder, you shall not commit adultery," he will not covet anything that belongs to his fellow, because, given that he knows that Hashem has provided his fellow and not himself with these items, he will realize that these are totally inaccessible to him. According to Ibn Ezra, *Lo sachmod* is not as much a commandment as a statement of fact. I.e., if one will observe the other commandments, *Lo sachmod* is a natural conclusion.

The *sefarim* discuss the mitzvah of *ve'ahavta es Hashem*, You shall love Hashem, and ask "How can one be commanded to love? Love is a feeling that is not subject to voluntary control."

Several approaches are suggested. Some cite the verse (*Proverbs* 27:19) that love is reciprocal. If a person emulates the Divine *mid-*

dos, one becomes close to Hashem, and Hashem's love for one gives rise to the reciprocal love for Hashem. R' Shneur Zalman in *Tanya* proposes the concept of "intellectual love"; i.e., when a person comes to the awareness that Hashem deserves to be loved, that fulfills the mitzvah of *ve'ahavta es Hashem*. The Baal Shem Tov said, "Develop *ahavas Yisrael*, love for your fellow Jew — and love for Hashem will follow."

The Torah tells us to love our fellow Jews and not carry hatred in our hearts. If we follow Torah guidelines to interpersonal relationships, the feeling of consideration for a fellow Jew will develop.

If we make the effort to refine our *middos*, we can indeed lessen the intensity of the animalistic traits within us. When the *yetzer hara* tries to debase you by telling you that you have sinful feelings, send it off by telling it that feelings are not sinful. You are responsible for your actions, and you will do your best to control them. You will do whatever is possible to increase your sensitivities, which will mitigate the intensity of some feelings, but you are not going to fall into the trap of feeling guilty for feelings that are part of your human nature.

Assuming Guilt

The *yetzer hara* is determined to cause trouble, and may do so under the guise of being a *tzaddik* who wants to set things right. It can quote Torah to serve its needs. That is why the Talmud warns us that the *yetzer hara* can distort Torah. As we previously mentioned, "If a person is meritorious, Torah becomes an elixir of life. If one is not meritorious, Torah becomes a lethal poison" (*Yoma* 72b).

While it is indeed important that we do a *cheshbon hanefesh*, a fearless moral inventory and own up to our shortcomings, it is equally important that we do not wrongly incriminate ourselves. *Sheker* (falsehood) is *sheker* under all circumstances. To consider oneself guilty when one is not guilty is a serious mistake.

Unwarranted guilt can depress a person. Whereas one can do *teshuvah* if one realizes that one has in fact done wrong, there is no *teshuvah* that can alleviate unwarranted guilt.

I have seen marriages destroyed by an abusive husband. Not only has the wife suffered years of abuse, but the effect on the children has been very detrimental. When she finally comes for help and is asked, "Why did you tolerate the abuse? Why didn't you go for help earlier?" she often says, "I felt that I was at fault and that I was not doing things right."

Any objective observer could see that she was being abused by a husband who was inconsiderate. Why was the wife unable to see this? I believe it is the work of the *yetzer hara*, causing her to find fault with herself, which permitted the abuse to continue and resulted in harm to her and the children.

King Solomon warns us, "Do not be overly righteous" (*Ecclesiastes* 7:18). Instead of recognizing that her husband's behavior was wrong, the woman is overly righteous, blaming herself.

True or False

The Talmud says that at the end of days, Hashem will slay the *yetzer hara*. The Baal Shem Tov asked, "Why will Hashem punish the *yetzer hara*? After all, it was simply doing the job for which it was created." The Baal Shem Tov answers, "Hashem created the *yetzer hara* to tell people to do *aveiros*, but the *yetzer hara* went far beyond his assignment, and misled people to think that *aveiros* are mitzvos. For that it deserves to be punished." truth

R' Dessler cites the *Chovos HaLevavos*, which states that the goal of the *yetzer hara* is to make *sheker* appear like *emes*. I have pointed out that low self-esteem is the result of the *yetzer hara* making one think that one is inferior, incompetent, and undeserving. It uses all its wiles to achieve that.

The power of truth is exceedingly great. We say in davening, "*Hashem Elokeichem emes*," Hashem *is* truth. Truth is a most potent weapon to defeat the *yetzer hara*. The Talmud relates that there was a town named Kushta (Aramaic for *emes*), whose inhabitants lived extraordinarily long lives. One time, a younger person died, and an investigation revealed that someone in the town had told a lie (*Sanhedrin* 97a). The Talmud informs us that Satan is the Angel of Death, and it could not take lives as long as truth prevailed. Thus, absolute adherence to truth repels Satan, and consequently also the *yetzer hara*.

Devotion to truth by repelling the *yetzer hara* can overcome its ability to delude a person by giving him a false self-image. Unfortunately, total devotion to truth is difficult to achieve. We often justify saying "white lies," but any falsehood will allow the *yetzer hara* to be effective. In the above Talmudic incident, we are told that the person was justified in not telling the truth, but this did not prevent its lethal effect.

Some of the *tzaddikim* were virtually fanatical in their adherence to *emes*. During World War I, R' Baruch Ber Lebovitz was returning from Russia to Poland. The border guards asked him if he was a citizen of Poland. His very life depended on his answer. R' Baruch Ber refused to lie, and said, "I am not a citizen of Poland, but I have students in Poland." The guards were impressed by his truthfulness and allowed him to enter Poland.

When R' Eliyahu Lopian served as *baal tefillah* (*chazzan*) on Rosh Hashanah, and said the introductory prayer of *Hineni he'ani* before Mussaf, he would skip the phrase, "trembling and frightened by the awesomeness of Hashem." He said, "How can I say that when I am not trembling with fear?"

R' Yechezkel Levenstein was a close friend of R' Yitzchak Eizek Scher. When the latter died, it was assumed that R' Yechezkel would eulogize him but R' Yechezkel refused, explaining, "Just a short while ago, I lost a dear grandchild, and I am in deep grief for him. If I eulogize R' Yitzchak Eizek, I may think of my grandson and cry. The audience will assume that I am crying in grief for R' Yitzchak Eizek, and that would not be the truth. I cannot give a false impression."

Remember, the *yetzer hara* is determined to destroy you, and its weapon is *sheker*. The *yetzer hara* will flee from *emes*. You can avoid its destructive influence by being uncompromising about truthfulness. I strongly urge reading R' Eliyahu Dessler's essay, "*Mabat HaEmes*" ("Perspective of Truth") in *Michtav MeEliyahu*, Vol.1.

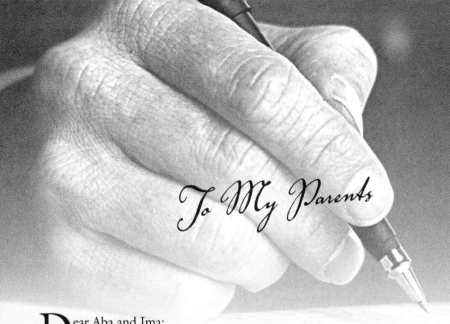

To My Parents

Dear Aba and Ima:

In psychotherapy, we may advise a client who is carrying resentments toward his deceased parents to write a letter to them expressing his feelings. Even though they will not read the letter, it may relieve the client's emotional heaviness.

If that works for resentments, it should also work for *hakaras hatov* (recognition of the good). We probably all fall short of adequately thanking our parents when they are alive. I was made aware that *hakaras hatov* is so important in *Yiddishkeit* that although we refer to Shavuos as *zeman matan Toraseinu* — the time of the Giving of our Torah — the Torah itself does not give Shavuos this designation. Rather, the Torah refers to Shavuos as *Yom HaBikkurim*, the day on which the farmer brings the first of his crops to the *Beis HaMikdash* and offers thanks to Hashem for the land and its produce. *Hakaras hatov* is given precedence.

Many years after I left Milwaukee, I received an invitation to attend a dinner hosted by the Maimonides Society of Wisconsin. Every year they give an award to the person who most typifies Rambam, and because I am a rabbi and a physician, I was chosen to receive the award. It seemed a bit absurd to me, because although I *am* a rabbi and a physician, I do not typify Rambam any more than a mosquito can be said to typify a 747 because they both fly.

At the dinner, they escorted a little old woman to the head table; I recognized her as Miss Wolski, my third-grade teacher in public school. She said, "Abraham, do you remember when you were the clown in the holiday play?" I said that I did. Miss Wolski said, "The week after that, your mother called, asking to meet with me. I realized I was in deep trouble for putting the rabbi's son in that play. When your mother came, all she wanted to know was whether I thought you were self-conscious because you were shorter than your classmates. I told her that I did not think so.

"Then I said to your mother, 'Mrs. Twerski, I was sure that you were going to reprimand me for putting Abraham in that play.' Your mother said, 'If what we have given him at home is not strong enough to resist the effects of a non-Jewish holiday play, then we have totally failed.'"

Ima, your words ring in my ears. I have to think, *What was it that you and Aba gave me that prevented me from being affected not only by that play, but also by eight years in a Catholic university and twenty years as Director of Psychiatry at St. Francis hospital? What was it that you and Aba gave me that rendered me resistant to the influences of philosophy and the non-Jewish concepts of psychology that I studied?* It is important for me to identify this, so that I can pass it on to my grandchildren.

What you gave us not only immunized us against the secular influences of public school, but has also enabled us to retain our *kedushah* in a society that has lost every vestige of *tzniyus.*

Of course, your abundant love for me was most important, but there had to be more than that.

Aba and Ima, you modeled for me the beauty of Torah *middos,* and especially *ahavas Yisrael.* Ima, although you were very learned, I saw how you related to the women in Milwaukee, none of whom had even a fragment of your knowledge. Yet you treated them all with great respect. Our house was open to everyone. Aba, you welcomed, befriended, counseled, and comforted everyone who consulted you. I remember that on Motza'ei Shabbos, right after *Havdalah,* you would phone any of the regular *mispallelim* who had not been in shul that day, to check if they were well. They felt, *From a whole shul full of people, the rebbe noticed that I was missing.* That gave them a feeling of worthiness.

Aba, you enabled me to feel the *simchah* of Torah and mitzvos. It is really regrettable that modern technology has taken away so much of the joy of mitzvos. I remember how, before Chanukah, you would buy a piece of beeswax, cut it into bits, soften them in hot water, flatten them, and using string as a wick, roll them into candles to serve as *shamashim.*Today I buy ready-made *shamashim.* Yes, it saves labor, but there is no fun in it.

There were no mass-produced Succah decorations, and we made all of ours by hand. We painted apples with bronze paint, and you wrote the appropriate *pesukim* on the wall. I never asked why a decorative bird was so important, for all the work you put into constructing one. Attaching the pleated colored paper to the empty eggshell with melted sealing wax was a work of art.

Aba, I remember the excitement of going out to the spring on Prospect Avenue on the afternoon before Erev Pesach to fetch water for baking the matzos the next day. I remember you looking at your pocket watch to tell us the precise moment at which we may fetch the water. We brought the water home and danced with the jugs on our shoulders. You made me realize that everything in *Yiddishkeit* is important, and everything warrants *simchah* as we fulfill Hashem's mitzvos. I feel so sorry for kids who don't have the opportunity to do this.

When I saw you put on *tefillin* I was reminded of the story behind these special, huge *tefillin*. For the sake of my great-grandchildren, I'm going to try to repeat the story you told me as accurately as I can.

> *After our ancestor, R' Nachum of Chernobyl, author of Meor Einayim, died, his wife would visit his colleagues, disciples of the Baal Shem Tov and the Maggid of Mezeritch, for consolation. One time, she visited R' Baruch of Medzhiboz, the grandson of the Baal Shem Tov, who said, "Tell me something about your holy husband."*
>
> *The Rebbetzin remained silent for a while, then abruptly rose and said, "I must leave here. After all the years I lived with my husband, I cannot think of anything to tell you. What is more, I cannot even recall his face. I take that as a sign that I don't belong here anymore."*
>
> *R' Baruch escorted the Rebbetzin to her coach, and just as the coachman was about to drive away, she stopped him.*

She said to R' Baruch, "I just thought of an incident of my husband. I would never relate this to anyone else, but inasmuch as I could not think of anything, and this memory did come to me, I take that as a sign that I should relate it.

"We lived in abject poverty. My husband had a pair of tefillin whose parshiyos had been written by R' Efraim Sofer, about whom the Baal Shem Tov said that next to Ezra HaSofer and Nechemiah HaSofer came R' Efraim Sofer. In Chernobyl, a wealthy man offered fifty rubles for the tefillin. Fifty rubles was then a great amount of money, but my husband refused to consider selling the tefillin.

"There were times when there was no food in the house and the children went to bed hungry. There were times when we shivered in the cold because we could not afford firewood. I said to my husband, 'For two rubles you can get a fine pair of tefillin, and with the balance we could support ourselves for two years. Don't you have any consideration for your children who are suffering from hunger and from the cold?' But my husband was adamant: The tefillin are not negotiable.

"I was raising my niece, Malkele, who was an orphan. I said to my husband, 'When we need to marry off Malkele and she will need a dowry, will you sell the tefillin?'

"My husband said, 'To marry off an orphan, one may even sell a sefer Torah.' This was my only consolation, that I would have a dowry for Malkele.

"One year, before Succos, my husband was very upset because there was no esrog available. Erev Succos, on his way home from shul, he noticed a man with an esrog and lulav.

He ran over to him and asked if the arba minim were for sale. The man said, 'Rebbe, this is way beyond your means. It is the only set in town. It is for the wealthy man, who is paying fifty rubles for it.'

"My husband said, 'Just wait here.' He reasoned, 'I don't need the tefillin for the next eight days. The esrog I need for the mitzvah tomorrow.'

He hurried to the home of the wealthy man, sold the tefillin, and for the fifty rubles, bought the arba minim.

"When I returned from the market, I saw that my husband was radiating simchah. Literally, the Shechinah was upon him. I asked him what was the cause of his great simchah, but he refused to tell me. But I kept pressing him, and finally he said that he had a set of arba minim for Succos. I asked, 'How could you possibly afford it?' and then he told me that he had sold the tefillin.

"When he told me that he had sold the tefillin, I recalled all the nights that the children went to bed hungry, shivering in the cold, but no, he would not sell the tefillin to feed the children and buy firewood, but he sold it for what? For a fruit that in eight days won't be worth a single kopek! And what about my Malkele's dowry? We would have nothing!

"I was overcome with rage. 'Where is the esrog?' I asked. He pointed to the cupboard. In my fury, I took the esrog and dashed it on the floor, whereupon the pitom was dislodged.

"My husband paled. Tears rolled down his cheeks. Very quietly, he said, 'The tefillin I no longer have. An esrog for Succos I no longer have. Now Satan would be pleased if I

> shouted at my wife and ruined the spirit of Yom Tov. I will
> not give him that satisfaction.'"
>
> R' Baruch remarked, "Rebbetzin, I can understand
> why your husband refused to sell the tefillin all those years. I
> can also understand why he did sell the tefillin to obtain an
> esrog. But how a human being can control oneself not to react
> in anger at such a moment — that is superhuman. Only a
> tzaddik like the Meor Einayim could do that."

These *tefillin* were later reclaimed and have been in the family
since.

Aba, I know that you told me this story to teach me that regardless
how aggravating circumstances may be, a person should never lose
control of his anger. I was reminded of this lesson each morning when
I saw you don the *tefillin*.

Restraining oneself when angry can be very difficult, but I had a
daily reminder that it can be done.

Aba, you also taught me a lesson about anger when someone
offended you. Some members of the shul were outraged and wanted to
ostracize him, but you said, "He doesn't understand that what he did
was foolish. I have to pity him for being a fool, and when I feel sorry
for someone, I can't be angry at him." I am grateful for this insight.

Aba, I've tried to emulate some of your *minhagim*. You would
serve as *shaliach tzibbur* during Minchah of Erev Rosh Hashanah. You
pointed out that if one davens this last Minchah of the year with full
kavannah, it can redeem all the faulty *Shemoneh Esreis* of the entire
year. Your *Shemoneh Esrei* was saturated with tears. Once, after this

Minchah, I heard some of the *mispallelim* say, "We are assured of having a good year. The Rebbe's prayers achieved this for us."

I can recall the morning *seudah* of Erev Yom Kippur, when you chanted the *selichos* of that morning, "*Yeratzeh tzom amcha*," asking Hashem to accept our fast as if it were a *korban* (sacrificial offering). "We are bereft of mitzvos, and lack the Kohen Gadol who can intercede for us ... Your children who have been banished from their homeland have gathered in Your house of worship. Remember for them the devotion of our ancestors as they stand in judgment before You." Sometimes I could not make out the words because your voice was washed away by your tears.

The Talmud says that if one eats on Erev Yom Kippur it is equivalent to a fast of two days (*Berachos* 8b). How can that be? I think that the Talmud was referring to the meal at which you sang *Yeratzeh tzom amcha*.

After this meal, Yom Kippur was actually anticlimactic, until *Ne'ilah*, for which you were the *shaliach tzibbur.* Your rendition of the *Shelosh Esrei Middos* (Thirteen Attributes of Mercy) was heartrending and unforgettable. I have tried to emulate you, but mine is only a weak imitation.

Aba, I recall that right after Yom Kippur, you called all the children and grandchildren to inquire how they fasted and to wish them a good year.

Although hundreds of people consulted you for advice, for any issues in the family you would say, "We must ask Ima's opinion."

The *sefarim* say that a person should eat only enough to obtain the nutrition necessary for optimal health so that one can serve Hashem, but not to indulge in gustatory delights. Is this possible in a society that is obsessed with food? I remember, Ima, that after Aba was gone, you said, "I lived with him for more than fifty years, but I never knew what foods he liked." Aba, you never expressed a preference or asked for any specific food; you were satisfied with whatever was served.

Ima, you have no idea how often I quote your wise words, such as "the holy *al tadin*," referring to the Talmudic statement "Do not judge your fellow until you have reached his place" (*Ethics of the Fathers* 2:5), or your quoting Rabbi Yisrael Salanter, "The trouble with our world is that everyone is concerned about his own *gashmiyus* (physicality); with regard to other people, their *ruchniyus* (spirituality) is his first priority." You had such wonderful interpretations of *Tehillim*, such as the verse, "Satisfy us in the morning with Your kindness, then we shall sing out and rejoice throughout our days" (*Psalms* 90:14), which you said meant that if in the morning — the early days of our life — we will be satiated with kindness, then we can be happy all our life.

Aba, I wish I inherited your upbeat attitude. You would come into a room, saying "*Lebedig, kinderlach, lebedig* (Be cheerful, children, be cheerful)."

Aba, you taught us not only how to live, but also how to die. Every Friday night, when you recited *Mizmor L'David* (*Psalm* 23) before *Kiddush,* you would say, "*Gam ki eilech begei tzalmaves, lo, lo, lo, lo ira ra ki attah imadi,* Even though I walk through the valley of the shadow of death, I will not, not, not, not fear evil because You are with me." I heard you say this every Friday night for decades. On the last Friday night of your life, when you recited, *"lo, lo, lo, lo ira ra ki attah imadi,"* you looked at me with a hint of a smile, which I interpreted to mean, "Now it's for real."

One of your last teachings, Aba, was your request that we not name children after you. You told me, "I love all my grandchildren, but there is a special place in my heart for the Ruchelach, who are named after my mother. Why set up a situation for favoritism?"

When you gave the same request to Aaron, you gave a different reason. You said, "I have had to mediate between two families, both of whom insist that a newborn child be named after a member of their family, and this causes totally unnecessary hard feelings. I cannot envision a new mother, in her sensitive state, crying because one of my children insists on naming the newborn child after me. This gives me no *kavod*."

I wondered why you gave Aaron a different reason than you gave me. I found out later, because Aaron had a son within the year of his father-in-law's death, and might have insisted that the child be named after you. With this message to Aaron, the problem was avoided.

But why did you not give that reason to me? No doubt because you somehow knew that I would not have more children after you were gone.

But of course, you know, Aba, that in this one area, we did not obey you, feeling that there was more *kavod* in giving the name than in not doing so, and that *Baruch Hashem*, we have many Yankelach.

The many stories you both told me about our *zeidies* and *bubbies* are priceless, and I try to convey them to your *einiklach*. These are rich sources of inspiration.

In my second year of medical school, a professor asked me what my plans were after medical school. I told him I was planning on becoming a psychiatrist. He said, "Good, good! Listen to all they teach you and give it back on the board examinations, then forget it all and use your head."

There was much of value that I learned in psychiatric training, but certainly your teachings helped prepare me. I was not aware that the stories you told me were a course in psychology.

Aba, I remember you told me about a man in Milwaukee who had earned the nickname *der krummer tzaddik* (the distorted *tzaddik*). He was opinionated and could not be budged. Then you told me this story:

> *When the first locomotive was introduced in Europe, word about this amazing phenomenon came to a small village. When the villagers heard that there was a wagon that moves without horses attached to it, they howled with laughter. "How stupid can people be to believe that a wagon will move without horses!"*
>
> *When more stories about the locomotive kept coming, the villagers decided that they must debunk this myth by a personal investigation. They chose the most enlightened person in the village to go to the big city and see what makes people believe that a wagon can move without horses.*
>
> *The representative returned and called a town meeting. "My friends," he said, "it is not a fantasy. It is true." He was greeted by derisive booing. When this subsided, he said, "Let me explain."*

He then drew on the board a diagram of the steam engine, showing how the fire turned the water to steam, which pushed up against a piston that was connected to wheels. Each time the steam pressure pushed against the piston, it caused the wheels to turn and the wagon to move.

A few of the villagers promptly understood, but many were bewildered. The representative then laboriously explained, with many diagrams, precisely how the steam engine worked. One by one, the villagers came around. There was only one stalwart who shouted at them, "Are all you people as crazy as the city people? For thousands of years, wagons never moved without horses, and now you believe there is some kind of magic that moves wagons without horses! We sent this man to the city, and the city people must have hypnotized him to believe in this fantasy, and you are foolish enough to go along with it!"

By this time the villagers had come around to understanding how the steam engine works, so they all ganged up on this man, each one demonstrating convincingly how steam pressure can push a piston that turns the wheels. After a long discussion, the stalwart finally said, "Oh! Now I see. Of course, the steam pushes the piston and it turns the wheels. How simple!"

Everyone breathed a sigh of relief. The representative then addressed the group. "Does anyone have any further questions?"

The stalwart raised his hand. "I understand everything perfectly: the steam pressure, the piston, the wheels. It's all very *clear. I have only one question: On the diagram you made of that wagon, just where do you hitch the horses?"*

An open-minded person may not grasp something at first, but with a bit of explanation will understand it. If, after adequate explanation a person still cannot understand your point, he probably has his mind made up and will not yield regardless of how convincing you may be. Instead of exhausting yourself in futility, just assume that he won't get it.

Ima, I must have been 5 years old when you told me the story that inspired my response in the following case history; I had not thought about it for more than forty years.

A young man consulted me. He was completing his first of three years in radiology residency, but was dissatisfied with this area of medicine. He was thinking about either psychiatry or pathology, and wanted my opinion about which to choose.

I said to myself, *That's strange. Psychiatry or pathology? You couldn't possibly get two specialties that are more polar opposites. Psychiatry requires intense interpersonal relationships, whereas pathology has none at all.*

The young man went on to say that prior to radiology he had been in an internal medicine program, but he was not happy with that.

This aroused my suspicion. I asked, "Before medical school, were you in any other field?" He told me that he had started engineering, but had dropped it because he was not pleased with it.

"How did you manage to stay in medical school?" I asked.

"My family would have killed me if I had quit," he said.

Then I remembered the story of the stonecutter.

> *The stonecutter earned his living hewing slabs of stone from a mountain. He often bewailed his sorry fate. "I have to work from dawn to dusk, breaking my back lifting this heavy pickaxe all day, and then I barely earn enough to put bread on the table for my family."*
>
> *One day he heard a loud tumult. Climbing to the peak of the mountain, he could see from afar that there was a parade in the city. The king was in a royal procession, and people had lined the streets shouting "Bravo! Long live the king!" and throwing flowers at the royal coach.*
>
> *The stonecutter raised his eyes to heaven. "Dear Lord," he said, "You are a just G-d. That king and I are both human beings. Where is the justice that he should be so mighty and powerful, and I should be so downtrodden? If You are indeed just, You will give me the opportunity to be as mighty as the king."*
>
> *Suddenly, he felt himself transformed. G-d had answered his prayer. He was the mighty king, receiving the accolades from thousands of loyal subjects. How thrilling it was to be so powerful!*
>
> *But then he began to feel very uncomfortable. Clad in his ermine robe, he was wilting as the sun's rays fell upon*

him. "What!" he said. "The sun can humble a king? Then the sun is most powerful. I wish to be the sun."

He was transformed into the sun, and enjoyed its unequaled power. But then he found himself frustrated. A dark cloud had passed beneath him and was not allowing his rays to go through.

"What!" he said. "A cloud can frustrate the sun? Then it must be mightier than the sun. I wish to be a cloud."

As a cloud he took great pleasure in frustrating the sun, but then a strong gust of wind blew him away. "The wind must be mightier than a cloud. I wish to be the wind."

As the wind, he became ferocious, causing tidal waves and leveling forests. But suddenly he was stymied. He had encountered a tall mountain that resisted his strongest gusts. "If a mountain is mightier than the wind, I wish to be a tall mountain."

As a tall mountain he dwarfed all else on earth, and felt most powerful. But then he felt a sharp pain. A stonecutter wielding a pickaxe was tearing away parts of him. He said, "If a stonecutter can dismantle a mountain, then he must be even mightier than the mountain. I wish to be that stonecutter."

And so he became the mightiest of all: a stonecutter.

I had not thought of that story until this young man told me how he was dissatisfied with everything he had tried. I told

— 129 —

him the story and said, "If you will be happy with yourself as a person, then you can be happy being an engineer or whatever kind of doctor you choose to be. If you are not happy with yourself, you can exhaust all the medical specialties and all the professions in the world and you will remain dissatisfied."

When I was 5 years old, I could not appreciate the wisdom in this bedtime story. It became apparent to me only forty years later.

A person with internal happiness can adjust to whatever position one attains. A person who seeks happiness in external sources may never be satisfied. He may be obstinately making constant changes in the expectation that he will find something to relieve his discontent. Each change brings but a fleeting relief, and he may exhaust himself in a futile search for happiness.

Aba, you taught me that mood may often depend on one's perspective rather than on the facts. You illustrated this with a story:

> In the villages of the old country, many people were illiterate. If they needed to write a letter, they would pay the town scribe to write it and to read the letters they received.
>
> One woman, whose son had immigrated to America, had not heard from him for several months. She asked the scribe to write him a letter, and she dictated the following:
>
> > Dear Son,
> > I'm sorry that I have not heard from you for several months. Please write me and let me know how things are going for you.

With me, things are quite well. We have had a difficult winter, and the cold wind would come in through the crevices in the wall. But thank G-d, I was able to seal the crevices with old garments. The price of food has gone up very high, but thank G-d, day-old bread is much cheaper. I can afford this and I don't go hungry. I still have my housecleaning job, and thank G-d that at my age I can still do this kind of work.

I am anxiously waiting to hear from you.

Love,

Mother

The woman then asked the scribe to read the letter back to her. The scribe, who was outraged at the son's neglect of his elderly mother, had written the following:

Dear Son:

What in the world is wrong with you that you have not written to me?

Conditions here are intolerable. The icy wind blows through the crevices in the walls, and I have to try to stuff them with rags. I can't afford proper food, and I have to survive on stale bread. In my old age I still have to get down on my hands and knees to scrub floors in order to survive. This is the kind of life I am leading here while you seem to be enjoying yourself in America.

I hope to hear from you soon.

Love,

Mother

— 131 —

When the scribe finished reading the letter, the woman grabbed her head with both hands and wailed, "Oh, no! I never knew how badly off I was until now!"

The same facts that had evoked her feelings of being fortunate now evoked feelings of misery. It is not the facts in life that make the difference, but how you look at them.

Ima, I'm sure you were not aware that you were preparing me to be a specialist in addiction. Here's the story you told me.

A poor man made a wish that he would have a purse which would never become empty. He found a magic purse that contained one dollar. When he removed the dollar, another appeared in its place. He was overjoyed that he would never be poor again, and kept on extracting dollars. Several days later he was found dead, lying atop of a huge pile of dollars.

Ima, I learned that this is the "happiness" of addiction.

For all of the above, Aba and Ima, and for much more, I am deeply grateful to you.

To My Children

"I have been diminished by all the kindnesses and all the truth that You have done for Your servant" (*Genesis* 32:11). Ramban says that the patriarch Jacob felt himself unworthy of all the kindnesses that Hashem had done for him.

Jacob could have attributed the kindnesses that Hashem had done for him to *zechus avos,* the merits of Abraham and Isaac, but he chose to see these as acts of *chesed*, kindnesses that were undeserved.

All the acts of the patriarchs are lessons for us. I am deeply grateful to Hashem for His abundant kindnesses in allowing me to have and enjoy a wonderful family. I could attribute this to *zechus avos.*

Bobbe (my mother) told me that when she was 5 years old, she saw the Zeide, R' Shloime (the first Bobover Rebbe), light the Chanukah menorah. He sat in front of the lit menorah, his eyes closed in meditation.

Bobbe asked him, "Zeide, what are you thinking about now?"

Zeide said, "I'm davening that you should have good children."

Bobtchu (Bobbe's mother) used to say to Bobbe, "You have no reason to worry about your children. You had a *berachah* from Zeide."

Indeed, the Talmud says that one who is careful about the Chanukah lights will have children who are Torah scholars (*Shabbos* 23b). Zeide's Chanukah lights have been a great *zechus* for our family.

I know that you have kept up the tradition of sitting at the Chanukah menorah for half an hour, saying the designated chapters of *Tehillim* seven times. I hope that this *zechus* will warrant that you have wonderful children and grandchildren.

I think it is appropriate that I ask *mechilah* (forgiveness). I was given the sacred trust of raising you, and I know that I have made mistakes. Even though my intentions were good, that does not exonerate me. It only makes me a *shogeig* (unintentional offender). Zeide used to quote the following Midrash:

> Adam asked Cain, "What kind of judgment did you receive?"
>
> Cain responded, "I did *teshuvah*, and I arrived at a settlement with my Maker."

Zeide asked, "Why only a 'settlement'? Doesn't *teshuvah* warrant total forgiveness?" He answered, "*Teshuvah* can achieve total forgiveness only if a sin does not have irreversible consequences. But Cain had killed Abel, who was not brought back to life. Therefore, Cain could not receive total forgiveness, but only a settlement."

Although I can't recall what they were, some mistakes that I made as a father might have left permanent scars on you. If so, *mechilah* cannot be absolute, only a "settlement."

Having said that, let me add that when clients attribute their problems to faulty parenting, I say to them, "Even if you are now what your parents made you, if you stay that way, it's your own fault." If you should consult a psychotherapist and discover how my parenting mistakes affected you, don't use them as grounds for feeling sorry for yourself. Being a victim is not in any way productive. We are capable of making great changes in ourselves, but we are creatures of habit, and there is much resistance to change. It is easier to blame, but blaming accomplishes nothing.

I am on record as saying, "When you bring a child into the world, you forfeit your rights to prioritize your own wants and needs. Everything you do should be in the interest of giving your child the best opportunity to be happy and productive. You may have to set your own wants and needs aside."

Yes, I did say that, but that was in the 1990's, when you were already parents and grandparents in your own right. I was not that wise in the 1950's, when you were born.

I am not immune to all the frailties that characterize a human being. I wish I had learned *Mishlei* when I was young, because King Solomon addresses these frailties. "Do not rely on your own understanding" (*Proverbs* 3:5), because "Every man's way is upright in his eyes" (ibid. 21:2). The Torah states, "… the bribe will blind the eyes of the wise" (*Deuteronomy* 16:19). When we have a desire for something, the *yetzer hara* deludes us to think that what we do to satisfy our desires is the right thing. We are subject to the "bribe" of our desires.

I cannot really take credit for the good that I have given you, because I was simply a passive agent in the transmission of a precious heritage. We had *zeidies* and *bubbies* of unparalleled greatness. When I would visit the Steipler Gaon, I would receive a royal welcome because I was a descendant of Zeide Reb Motele.

Of course, *yichus* is a double-edged sword. As the *Shelah HaKadosh* says, *yichus* commits you to a higher standard of behavior.

Babba Sarah Marium suffered from Alzheimer's disease in her advanced age, and she would say, "I don't know who I am or where I am, but I do know *whose* I am." You should never lose sight of whose you are.

In an important essay by the Rebbe of Slonim in *Nesivos Shalom* (Vol. 1, pp. 18-21), the Rebbe identifies "the essential Jew."

One may be a Jew because one was born to Jewish parents or because one underwent conversion. This does not make one an "essential" Jew. One may be observant of all the mitzvos, but this only makes him a Jew *by his conduct*. To be a Jew "of essence," one's Jewishness must be ingrained in one's very being, in one's mind and heart and in every organ of one's body. All one's ideation and perspectives must be Jewish, and one's emotions and desires must be Jewish. One's natural cravings must be Jewish, limited and restrained by the awareness that the Holy One is within him.

One must have an awareness that one is a member of the *am hanivchar* (chosen people). Prior to giving the Torah at Sinai, Hashem said, "Tell the House of Jacob and the Children of Israel, 'You saw what I did to Egypt, and I lifted you on the wings of eagles and brought you to Me. And now, if you will listen to My voice and observe My covenant, you will be to Me a treasure from among all the nations. Because to Me belongs all the Earth. And you will be unto me a kingdom of priests and a holy nation'" (*Exodus* 19:3-6).

At this point, Hashem has not mentioned specific mitzvos, but the concepts cited are prerequisites to receiving the Torah. The mitzvos were given to people who are Jews "in essence," and the concepts tell us what it means to be a Jew "in essence." Therefore, Hashem said, "You saw that I delivered you from Egypt and elevated you to a higher level than the heavenly angels, because angels are My servants, whereas you are My children." A Jew "in essence" must always remember that one is a child of Hashem.

Then Hashem said, "You will listen to My voice." He had not yet commanded mitzvos. "Listening to My voice" means accepting Hashem's authority. A Jew "in essence" must realize that Hashem is constantly speaking to him. "The heavens declare the glory of Hashem and the firmament tells of His handiwork (*Psalms* 19:2). Everything in nature testifies to Hashem as the Creator Who conducts the world. To "observe My covenant" is the bond of love and devotion to Hashem. A "Jew in essence" is constantly aware of the intimate relationship between Hashem and Israel, and is cautious not to do anything that might weaken that bond.

A "Jew in essence" must constantly be aware that one is the bearer of a *neshamah* that is part of Hashem, and that one is, therefore, of inestimable value. Being a "Jew in essence" enables a person to properly fulfill the mitzvos.

Tzaddikim have said that the worst of all sins is to forget that one is a child of Hashem, and that Hashem's love for every Jew is incalculable. The Baal Shem Tov said, "I wish I could have the love for the greatest *tzaddik* that Hashem has for the worst *rasha*."

King David had a rebellious son, Absalom, whose behavior was despicable, and who pursued his father to kill him. David told his officers to quell the revolt, but to be careful to spare Absalom. When David found out that Absalom had been killed, he wept inconsolably. "My son, Absalom! My son, my son, Absalom! If only I could have died in your place! Absalom, my son, my son!" (*II Samuel* 19:1). Hashem's love of even sinful Jews is greater even than David's love of his rebellious son.

When we say in our davening, "Who loves His nation, Israel," we should concentrate with *kavannah* on the love Hashem has for every Jew, and this should give one a sense of *chashivus*.

As noted above, the *mussar* authority, R' Simchah Zissel Ziv, commenting on the verse in *Psalms* (118:13), "*Dacho dechisani linpol, vaHashem azarani,* They pushed me hard that I might fall, but Hashem assisted me," states that *dacho* refers to the crushing force *that is inherent in human nature, which tries to topple a person to the ground by making one feel worthless.*

R' Simchah Zissel's interpretation of *dacho dechisani linpol* is of enormous importance. It draws attention to the powerful force of the *yetzer hara*, and that the only way to resist its destructive force is *vaHashem azarani*, with the help of Hashem. This means not only by *tefillah* but by living in a way that brings one close to Hashem, being a "Jew in essence" and observing the mitzvos. It is important to note that although observance of mitzvos is paramount, *Nesivos Shalom* refers to this as "a Jew in conduct," which is not yet "a Jew in essence."

Do not lose sight of the fact that the goal of the *yetzer hara* is to crush you. It may do so by telling you how unworthy you are, reminding you of the *aveiros* you committed or your laxity in Torah and mitzvos. If you get into a discussion or argument with the *yetzer hara* and become defensive, it will defeat you. The proper response is, "Yes, I have committed sins, but that was in the past. I am now dedicated to *teshuvah*, which will erase those sins and bring me closer to Hashem."

Never lose sight of "whose you are."

I don't think a parent can have a greater *nachas* than seeing all his children relating with mutual love. Many families are unfortunately fragmented, often because of pettiness. Not too long ago, I was at a wedding together with my brothers, Reb Michel and Reb Aaron, when a man approached us and said, "Three brothers getting along amiably is not normal!"

I am so grateful to Hashem to see my family getting along well with one another.

May Hashem bless you as He has blessed me, with great *nachas*.

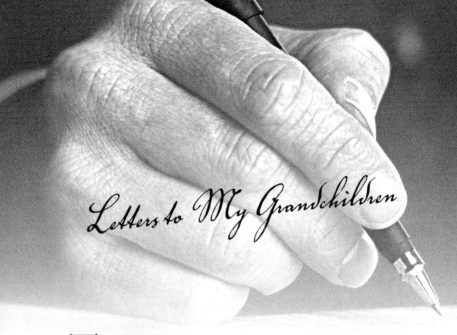

Letters to My Grandchildren

These letters were written at different times, and given the importance of several thoughts I want to pass on to the future generations, I do not doubt that there may be some repetition. Truthfully, I don't think that is detrimental; rather, it is a sign that these opinions and emotions are primary in order to conduct oneself as an *ehrliche Yid*.

Although the letters were directed to a *chassan* (bridegroom) and *kallah* (bride), the content of each is universal and can be of benefit to everyone, and therefore I am certain the reader will enjoy and profit from them.

To My Grandson, the Chassan:
A Grandfather's Guide to Marriage

My dear grandson:

Mazal tov on your engagement! *Baruch Hashem*, you have been blessed with a lovely *kallah* who comes from a beautiful family. You have been studying Torah diligently, and I know you to have fine *middos* (character traits). You should have a blissful marriage. May Hashem bless you both with the fulfillment of your hearts' desires.

I am writing to you because I have often been consulted by couples who likewise could have been expected to have a blissful marriage, but unfortunately, things did not turn out that way. I have come to realize that even with the finest family backgrounds, and even where the young man and woman were excellent students in yeshivah and seminary respectively, there are many possible pitfalls in marriage.

I am also writing to your cousin who recently became a *kallah*. You should read both letters, because there are some important points in each that apply to both husband and wife.

Many factors essential to a good marriage are well known. However, as Ramchal says in *Mesillas Yesharim* (*Path of the Just*), it is precisely those things that are familiar to us that we may take for granted and consequently we do not give them adequate attention. We know that being considerate is most important in a relationship. But just what does it mean to be considerate? It is possible for people to assume that they are considerate even though they may be lacking in this important trait.

I feel that many young men and women are simply not prepared well for the responsibilities of marriage and parenthood. Consequently, when stresses in these areas occur, they are at a loss how to deal with them properly.

In the Torah world, when young men become engaged, they learn the halachos pertaining to marriage. However, all too often, no one teaches them the ABC's of relationships.

Perhaps it was not all that essential for such guidance to be given in the past, but we are living in a different world today. Moral values have fallen by the wayside, and hedonism has become the prevailing philosophy of life. The sanctity and strength of the traditional Jewish family have weakened. Attitudes totally alien to *Yiddishkeit* bombard us from all sides. The street is a toxic place, and some of the toxicity penetrates even our closed doors. We must have better preparation for marriage and family life.

The relationship of husband to wife is unlike any of your other relationships. You have never experienced this type of bond before.

This is why I feel that guidance in this uniquely new connection is essential. This relationship is different from that of child to parent or that of friend to friend. Children and parents, friends and friends, are distinct from one another, regardless of how close they may feel. Of husband and wife, however, the Torah says, "they shall become one flesh" (*Genesis* 2:24). The Torah requires that a husband consider his wife as part of him. He should relate to her with the same care that he gives any other part of his person.

In fact, the Talmud states, "One should love his wife as much as he loves himself, and respect her even more than he respects himself" (*Yevamos* 62b). The Talmud thus extends the consideration for one's wife beyond that which one grants himself.

This may be a good point to introduce several other passages in the Talmud that pertain to the husband-wife relationship. Remember, these are as binding upon us as are any other halachos. One who is meticulously observant of other halachos but is remiss in observance of the Talmudic teachings about the marriage relationship is derelict in Torah observance.

We would not think of a person who eats butter-fried chicken as being Torah observant; neither should we consider a person who is derelict in following the Talmudic teaching of the husband-wife relationship as being Torah observant. It is unfortunate that some people place greater emphasis on ritual observance than on the quality of their relating to other people.

To emphasize this point, I present you with this story.

In Vilna, a shoemaker inherited great wealth and thereby achieved the local prominence often accorded to the wealthy.

When he married off his daughter, there was an impressive
procession from his home to the courtyard of the shul, where
the wedding ceremony was to take place.

One local citizen was jealous of the shoemaker's rise to
prominence. In the midst of the wedding procession, the man
approached the shoemaker and attempted to hand him a
pair of shoes. "Do you think you can have these repaired by
tomorrow?" he asked.

R' Yisrael of Salant was appalled by this public
humiliation. He said, "After this event, the previous rabbis
of Vilna were called from Gan Eden to stand in judgment
before the Heavenly Tribunal. They were being held
responsible for not having sufficiently impressed upon the
populace the importance of proper middos, which would have
prevented the occurrence of a public humiliation."

The preservation of human dignity is of great importance, sometimes overriding a conflicting halachah (see *Berachos* 19b). Think of
it this way: A person who is very hungry is unable to control himself
and goes into a McDonald's and eats a cheeseburger. He has committed a grave sin by frankly violating a Torah restriction, and he will
be judged for this by the Heavenly Tribunal. However, this does not
detract from the reward he may have earned by the study of Torah
(*Sotah* 21a). On the other hand, a person who was diligently observant of Torah from childhood on, at the age of 84 humiliates someone publicly and does not apologize. Even if he has Torah and good
deeds to his credit, he has no share in *Olam Haba* (*Ethics of the Fathers*
3:15). The Chofetz Chaim adds that this is true even if the humili-

ation occurs in private. Such is the importance the Talmud gives to human dignity.

Obviously, the dignity of one's spouse is no exception. There is never any justification to disrespect one's spouse.

Let us now turn to Talmudic statements that affirm this concept.

> A person must always be careful about his wife's honor, because blessing is found in one's home only on account of his wife. As it is stated, "And He treated Abram well on her [Sarah's] account" (*Genesis* 12:16; *Bava Metzia* 59a).

Let us weigh the Talmud's words carefully. We can hardly think of anyone who could possibly surpass the spiritual greatness of the patriarch Abraham. Yet the Talmud says that the Divine blessings are bestowed by virtue *only* of the wife. Your study of Torah and observance of mitzvos, my dear grandson, are of inestimable value. But remember, the Divine *berachah* is accorded in your wife's merits rather than your own.

> A person must always be wary of verbally wronging his wife, for since her tears come easily, the punishment for wronging her is nearby; i.e., not long in coming (*Bava Metzia* 59a).

The Talmud states that because a woman is exquisitely emotionally sensitive, great care must be taken to ensure that she is not upset.

> *The Talmud relates that R' Rechumi was diligent in his Torah study in the academy of Rava, returning home Erev Yom Kippur. One time, R' Rechumi was so deeply engrossed in Torah study that he was late in returning home. His*

wife awaited his return anxiously. "He is coming soon, he is coming soon," she repeatedly said to herself. When he did not come, she was distressed and a tear dropped from her eye. R' Rechumi was sitting in an attic at the time. The attic gave way beneath him and he died (Kesubos 62b).

So harsh a judgment for a single tear! And why was R' Rechumi late? Because he was studying Torah. Truly an amazing *gemara*.

Do not relate to your wife according to your own standards. You may be indifferent to things that may cause her distress. You may not give any significance to your birthday, and you might not care in the least whether or not she remembered it. But if your wife would feel slighted if you do not remember her birthday, you must make sure to remember it. Make note of days that may be important to her, especially her birthday and your anniversary.

I am annoyed when poorly informed people sometimes cast groundless aspersions, saying that Torah favors men above women. They cite the fact that men have more mitzvos and are, therefore, more privileged. Throughout my lifetime, I have heard the Kohanim preface their *berachos* (blessings) by saying, "G-d has sanctified us with the *kedushah* (holiness) of Aaron." Not once have I felt inferior to Kohanim by my inability to join them in pronouncing the *berachos* nor that I am not as sanctified as they are! Each person has his or her unique place in Judaism, and each should be satisfied with the position in which G-d has placed him or her.

In sports, a team is supposed to do its utmost to win. Each player has a specific assignment. Players on a baseball team are assigned their positions by their ability and the judgment and decision of the manager.

Can you imagine an outfielder protesting his position and insisting that he wants to be the pitcher because the latter receives more media exposure? Each player has his role and is of equal importance to the team. Any individual player who puts his own career ahead of the team interest is a detriment to the team.

Our Manager has assigned roles to Kohanim, Levites, and Israelites, to women and to men. *Klal Yisrael* is a team. A woman who feels underprivileged fails to understand this. Men who consider themselves superior to women are equally in error.

There are those who may be in error, and unfortunately, this misconception may sometimes be found even in people of authority. This is not a new phenomenon. The Talmud relates that when the daughters of Zelophehad heard that the tribal portions of Eretz Yisrael were to be allotted to the males through the paternal line, they took counsel and said, "G-d's compassion is not like that of humans. Humans are more considerate of males than of females. The Creator is not like that. His consideration is for both males and females, for it is written (Psalms 145:9), 'He is good to all; His mercies are on all His works'" (*Sifri Pinchas* 27).

We are commanded to emulate Hashem. "Just as He is merciful, so you should be merciful. Just as He is gracious, so you should be gracious" (*Shabbos* 133b). Anyone who lacks this impartiality is derelict in the commandment to emulate Hashem.

How thrilling it is to study Torah! There is little that can compare to the brilliance of the *Chiddushei HaRim*, the clarity of the *Ketzos HaChoshen*, or Reb Chaim's analysis and reconciliation of conflicting rulings of Rambam. To whom do we owe all of this?

The Talmud states that the Jewish Torah world had become barren and that Torah would have been forgotten had it not been that the great R' Akiva restored it by teaching it to R' Meir, R' Shimon bar Yochai, R' Yose ben Chalafta, R' Yehudah bar Ila'i, and R' Nechemiah (*Yevamos* 62b). Torah was saved from extinction by R' Akiva, and we owe all our Torah knowledge to him.

> *As we know, R' Akiva was still illiterate at age 40, and it was only at the behest of his wife, Rachel, that he left Jerusalem to learn Torah. She sacrificed his company for 24 years so that he could excel in Torah. She cut off and sold her beautiful hair to support his learning.*
>
> *When he returned home with thousands of disciples, Rachel came to greet him. Not knowing who she was, R' Akiva's students blocked her access to the master. R' Akiva said to them, "Let her come. Everything that I know in Torah and everything you know in Torah we owe to her" (Kesubos 62b-63a).*

The next time you are enthralled with Torah, remember your obligation to Rachel.

As I watch yeshivah students davening *Shemoneh Esrei*, meditating, and silently verbalizing the *tefillah* (prayer), I cannot but wonder whether they are aware that we know the most about *tefillah* because of Chanah, the mother of the prophet Samuel (*Berachos* 31b).

You are familiar with the Midrash that we merited liberation from the bondage of Egypt only by virtue of the righteous women (*Sotah* 11b). You also remember that not a single woman participated in the worship of the Golden Calf, a sin that has cast its shadow over our entire painful history. And after the spies returned with a negative

— 148 —

report about the Promised Land and the lamentation of the Israelites caused a calamity from which we still suffer today, it was the men who demanded that Moses be deposed and a new leader appointed to lead them back to Egypt. It was the women who insisted on proceeding to the conquest of Canaan (*Rashi, Numbers* 26:64).

When Jerusalem was destroyed and we were driven into exile, the patriarchs Abraham, Isaac, and Jacob pleaded to G-d for mercy for their children, but their pleas were not effective. Moses, whose supplication for Divine compassion had never before been turned away, was equally unsuccessful. It was only the intervention of the matriarch Rachel that elicited the Divine response, "It is only by your merit, Rachel, that your children will be returned to their homeland" (Introduction to *Eichah Rabbah*).

Certainly you will wish your children to be Torah scholars. The groundwork for their success in Torah will be provided by your wife rather than by you. Solomon says, "Hearken, my son, to the discipline of your father, and do not forsake *the Torah of your mother*" (*Proverbs* 1:8). It will be her emotional input in their infancy that will prepare them for your teaching. Indeed, at Sinai, in giving Moses the instructions on receiving the Torah, the women are mentioned before the men (*Exodus* 19:3).

For everything precious to us — our liberation, our Torah knowledge, our *tefillah*, and the ultimate Redemption — we are indebted to women. Little wonder that the Talmud accords the wife so lofty a status. It can only be crass ignorance that can lead to failure to appreciate the overriding role of the woman in Judaism.

But does the Torah not state that the man shall rule over the wife (*Genesis* 3:16)? It is evident from all our Torah ethical works that in this case the word "rule" means that the husband should be the *titular* head of the family. The husband sits at the head of the table, makes *Kiddush*, and recites the *HaMotzi* over the challah for the family. This verse does not give a husband the right to be dictatorial or tyrannical.

Halachah requires that husband and wife respect each other. Rambam describes how the husband should respect his wife and how the wife should respect her husband (*Hilchos Ishus* 15:19-20). In your study of Rambam, you have been taught to pay close attention to every nuance in his great work. It is not only the content of the halachah that is important, but also just where each particular halachah has been placed. It is, therefore, noteworthy that Rambam placed the halachah of the husband's duty to respect his wife *before* that of the wife's respect for her husband. Of course, both are of equal importance and should be concurrent. However, if anyone questions where the respect should begin, the Rambam's sequence provides the answer.

Even in the finest of relationships there are bound to be disagreements, but you must be careful how you disagree. We can learn this from the Torah decree that one must respect one's parents. If one's father is doing an action that seems to be a transgression, one may not chastise him. Rather, halachah states that one must politely ask, "Father, is it not written in the Torah that this is not permissible?" Halachah teaches us how to disagree without being disrespectful.

Inasmuch as we have seen that the Talmud requires that a husband respect his wife even more than himself, disagreeing must be done respectfully. No shouting, no denouncing, and certainly never using any derogatory or insulting terms.

Calm, gentle disagreement is not only necessary to fulfill one's duty to be respectful, but it is also wise and practical. When you raise your voice in argument, your opponent becomes defensive. His attitude immediately changes from being receptive to what you are saying to thinking of how to counterattack. He tunes you out and may not even hear what you are saying. I have observed altercations in couples and have noted that they are often talking past each other. Neither has really heard the other.

If what you say has substance, say it quietly. You will make your point. Solomon says, "The gentle words of the wise are heard above the shouts of a king over fools" (*Ecclesiastes* 9:17). If you feel like shouting, pause for a moment and rethink what you are about to say. Chances are you will find that your "argument" is very weak.

I heard a charming comment from a man who said, "I used to argue with my wife. I didn't want to lose an argument. But if I won, that meant that she lost. *But I didn't want to be married to a loser.* So we stopped arguing."

Differences of opinion can be sensible discussions. They do not have to be arguments.

King Solomon writes, "A man's every way is upright in his eyes" (*Proverbs* 21:2). This is a psychological fact. We are generally oblivious of our own character defects. If others point them out to us, we may question their motives and doubt the validity of their criticism.

Many people have difficulty accepting constructive criticism. Solomon calls them fools and scoffers. "A scoffer does not like his being reproved; he will not go to the wise" (ibid., 15:12). "An understanding heart will seek wisdom, and the mouth of fools will befriend folly" (ibid., v. 14). Speaking softly and meaning well instead of instigating a quarrel may lead to your comments being more readily accepted.

Hashem, in His infinite goodness, provided man with an *ezer kenegdo*; literally, "a helper corresponding to him" (*Genesis* 2:18). That is, someone who can help him but who can stand in opposition to him if necessary. A devoted wife is indeed one with her husband, yet she can stand aside and be more objective. Your wife may see *middos* that you need to correct of which you may be unaware. Her bringing these to your attention is Hashem's special gift to you. A husband who reacts with negativity to his wife's criticism is not only losing the opportunity to improve himself, but is also rejecting Hashem's kindness.

At times it may be that young men do not know how to relate properly to their wives because they have not had the best role models. Regrettably, parents do not always provide the best examples. Many yeshivah boys look up to their Torah teachers and consciously or unconsciously emulate them, but there is one important aspect of the rebbi's behavior that they do not observe. They have virtually no opportunity to see how their rebbi relates to his wife. Most of the accounts we have about the lives of our great Torah personalities were written by their students or chassidim. Not many children were their parents' biographers. Children could have described how their parents related to each other. Unfortunately, there is a great void in this area.

In our generation we were privileged to have a Torah giant whose *middos* were exemplary. I suggest you read a biography of R' Shlomo Zalman Auerbach, a *gaon* and *tzaddik* whom I was privileged to know. There are many stories of how he ingeniously managed to respect the dignity of others even when there were halachic problems. He never transgressed halachah and never embarrassed anyone.

R' Shlomo Zalman was traveling on a bus (he felt that it was not proper to take a taxi at the yeshivah's expense) when an immodestly clad woman boarded and sat next to him. He waited a few moments, then signaled for a stop, and, with a smile, said to her, "Pardon me, but I must get off here." He stepped off the vehicle and waited for the next bus. An onlooker asked why he had done this.

R' Shlomo Zalman replied, "What else could I do? I could not continue to sit there. If I had moved to another seat, I would have insulted her. Just because she does not dress with tzniyus (modesty) I don't have the right to humiliate her."

R' Shlomo Zalman was a *gadol* in *middos* as well as in halachah.

When R' Shlomo Zalman's wife died, he said, "It is customary to ask mechilah (forgiveness) from the departed person for any offense one might have committed toward them. We lived our lives according to the Torah, so there is really nothing for which I must ask mechilah. Nevertheless, since it is a minhag, I will comply with it."

Can you imagine this? A person has lived with another person in a close relationship for some sixty years and is secure in the knowledge that he never offended her, even once in sixty years! This would be difficult to believe of anyone except for R' Shlomo Zalman.

"We lived our lives according to the Torah," and that is why there was no need to ask *mechilah*. This was not the aspect of the Torah that deals with Shabbos or *kashrus*. This was the aspect of the Torah that deals with proper behavior between man and wife. Many people may truthfully state, "I never ate *tereifeh* all my life," or "I never missed a single day of putting on *tefillin*." How many people can truthfully say, "During many years of marriage, I never offended my spouse"? To R' Shlomo Zalman, the Torah guidelines for proper behavior toward a wife were of no less importance than the laws of Shabbos and *kashrus*. This is what it means to lead a Torah-true life.

> *A woman came to R' Aryeh Levin and complained that her husband was abusive. She asked the rav to please speak to him about this. R' Aryeh told her that if he were to chastise the husband, he might become even more abusive toward her for having reported him.*
>
> *"I will have an opportunity to speak about this without revealing that you had spoken to me," he said.*
>
> *R' Aryeh would teach Ein Yaakov between Minchah and Maariv, and this man regularly attended these sessions. When R' Aryeh came to a portion that discussed relationships, he elaborated emphatically and at great length on the Torah requirements for respecting one's wife and how harsh the Divine punishment is for causing her distress.*
>
> *R' Aryeh's teacher and mentor, the great gaon and tzaddik R' Isser Zalman Meltzer, happened to be in the shul at the time. He said to R' Aryeh, "I must express my gratitude for your lecture today. I have not thought enough about whether I am observing the Torah requirements for respecting my wife properly. Your lecture has reminded me that I must do some soul-searching."*

Why is it that those people who need it the least hear it the most?

You should realize that although your wife loves you very much, you are nevertheless a newcomer in her life. For the past two decades her relationships have been with her parents, siblings, and extended family. These relationships are very dear to her and you should respect them.

As a Torah scholar you remember that the Torah says, "Therefore a man shall leave his father and mother and cleave unto his wife" (*Genesis* 2:24). Note that it does not say the reverse. Apparently it is easier for a man to detach from his family than it is for a woman to do so.

Some men, probably because of feelings of inferiority, may misinterpret the wife's desire to be with her family as reflecting a lack of love for him. *If she really loves me, why would she still need to be with her family that much?* It is foolish to make an unreasonable demand for the wife to have no other needs in the world except for the relationship with her husband. I have seen ego-crazed, controlling husbands who demanded virtual worship and unquestioning obedience from their wives.

There are some generally accepted customs for newlyweds, such as with which family the young couple will spend the first Seder after their marriage. Regardless of what the custom is, be sensitive to your wife's needs. Remember, the Talmud says that her emotional needs are greater than yours.

Never, but never belittle your wife's family. Remember, she loved and respected them long before she loved and respected you. If you think you are going to gain in stature by belittling them, you could not possibly be more wrong. The Talmud says that an honorable person is one who *gives* respect (see *Ethics of the Fathers* 4:1), rather than one who *receives* honors.

The demand that "Things must be done my way" has ruined many marriages.

Zeide was very dedicated to his heritage. Nevertheless, he sang *Shalom Aleichem* the way Bobbe's father did rather than how his own father had. He also adopted a number of other practices of his father-in-law. This was not only to assuage her homesickness, but also to indicate that he valued her family's *minhagim*. This is just a minute example of Zeide's sensitivity and consideration for Bobbe.

This relationship with your wife is very new to you. Keep that in mind. There are many things you will learn as you go along. As long as you are sensitive and considerate, you will integrate this new knowledge.

I have every reason to believe that your marriage will be blissful. You and your *kallah* have found each other by a method that has been in our family and culture for many centuries. However, the rationale for this method must be understood so that it can result in a happy marriage.

In Western civilization, marriages are based on what is referred to as "love." A young man and young woman "fall in love" and decide to marry. The fact that the incidence of failed marriages is so high in this culture should raise some eyebrows. What is the flaw in this method?

> *The Rebbe of Kotzk once saw a young man obviously enjoying a dish of fish. "Why are you eating the fish?" the Rebbe asked.*
>
> *The young man looked puzzled. "Why? Because I love fish, of course," he said.*
>
> *"Oh," the Rebbe said, "and it was because of your love for*

the fish that you took it out of the water, killed it, and cooked it. That is a strange way to show your love.

"The reason you did that, young man," the Rebbe continued, "is not because you love the fish. What you love is yourself. Because of your self-love, you wish to satisfy your appetite. The fish tastes good to you, so you killed it for your own gratification. There is nothing wrong with that. Just do not delude yourself that you love the fish."

The Rebbe of Kotzk made an excellent point. Much of what Western civilization calls "love" is not really the love of another person, but rather self-love, "fish-love," if you will.

A young man and a young woman meet. He feels that she can provide for all his emotional needs, and she feels that he can provide for her emotional needs. This is called "falling in love." There is indeed a love relationship, but it is essentially self-love.

A marriage based on self-love is on unsteady ground. Suppose that after some time the man thinks that there is another woman who can better provide for his emotional needs. If self-love is the cement of the relationship, it stands to reason that he may wish to terminate the first relationship. Also, infatuation may blind the young people to major disparities in their outlook on life. When this phase passes, incompatibilities may come to the surface.

The advantage of a *shidduch* (arranged marriage) is that both partners usually come from similar backgrounds, and this may eliminate areas of ideological conflict. Limited contact prior to the engagement reduces the possible distortion of judgment due to infatuation. However, even in the best of situations the young man, the young woman, or both might enter the marriage with his or her own agenda. Self-interest may still be a dominant factor, and frustration in gratifying that self-interest may cause difficulties in the relationship.

Couples who seek marriage counseling are often told that their problem is one of communication: They are not communicating well to each other. That may be true, but I suspect that the cause is not always faulty communication.

One time when at the airport, I was standing near a man on the moving walkway. He recognized someone on the adjacent moving walkway, which was going in the opposite direction. They exchanged a few words, but were soon out of communication range. These people may both have had excellent communication skills. The reason their communication failed was because they were heading in opposite directions.

If a young man is primarily interested that the marriage relationship should provide for *his* needs, and the young woman is interested that the marriage provides fulfillment of *her* needs, the two may be heading in different directions. There is no common goal that sets them on the same path.

At the wedding ceremony, the first *berachah* after the giving of the ring is *shehakol bara lichvodo*, which states that Hashem created everything for His glory. This is indeed a wonderful concept, but what is its relevance to marriage?

I believe that the Sages instituted this *berachah* to tell the young couple that they have a common goal. Their primary function should be to establish a family that will bring honor to the Name of Hashem.

The Talmud gives us the formula for this. "If a person transacts business honestly and behaves respectfully, people will say, 'How fortunate are the parents who bore him, and how fortunate is the teacher who taught him Torah'" (*Yoma* 86a). Establishing a family that manifests the high ethics of Torah is a *kiddush Hashem*. That is the couple's foremost responsibility and constitutes the principal reason for marriage.

of the act

There is no denying that the emotional needs of both husband and wife should be met. However, if these are the primary basis for the marriage and they are frustrated, the relationship may falter. If the prime purpose is *shehakol bara lichvodo,* there is a firm basis for the relationship that can enable it to sail through stormy seas.

A healthy marriage can exist only when there is mutual trust between husband and wife. Concealing or withholding important information will be ruinous to the relationship. Of course, information that was shared in confidence must not be made public, and both partners should understand why they must respect a confidence. I do not refer to secretive actions or moral and ethical failings that will destroy a marriage. However, withholding information that the other spouse has every right to know undermines the trust that is so vital in a marriage.

Of course, the rules of *lashon hara* must be observed. A husband or wife may hear a juicy piece of gossip and just can't wait to get home to tell it to the spouse. The restrictions against *lashon hara* apply within the family as well. If the husband hears something and then discovers that his wife knew about it three weeks ago, he may ask, "Why didn't you tell me?" She should reply, "Because it's *lashon hara.*"

One of the problems I come across with some frequency is when a parent calls and asks, "My son/daughter is 20. Two years ago he/she was treated for depression/obsessive-compulsive disorder/ panic disorder, etc. He/she has recovered. We are involved in *shidduchim* now. Am I obliged to reveal his/her past problem? If I do, it may ruin the chance of a *shidduch*."

I not only empathize with the parents, but I agonize with them. I don't believe one must tell the *shadchan*, and it is not necessary to reveal this on the first date. However, if it seems that the *shidduch* may progress, I firmly believe that the prospective match must be told: *There is something I must share with you. I had this problem for which I was treated.* If the person is still being medicated, this too must be revealed. It is unthinkable to enter a relationship as intimate as marriage with deception. Every *posek* I have consulted has said that it is obligatory to reveal such information.

Poskim have told me that the Chofetz Chaim, the greatest authority on *lashon hara*, says that if someone knows that a party to a pending *shidduch* had a condition, which, if known to the other side, would cause them to rethink going forward with the *shidduch*, *one is obligated to reveal such information even if not asked*! Failure to do so violates the commandment, "*Lo saamod al dam re'acha*, You shall not stand aside while your fellow's blood is shed" (*Leviticus* 19:16).

The parents are understandably reluctant to reveal anything that would jeopardize the success of the *shidduch*. I ask them, "How would you feel if the situation were reversed? What would you say if after your son/daughter was married, it was discovered that significant information had been withheld?" Even though they realize that they would feel deceived, they still may not be able to force themselves to reveal the potentially damaging information.

I know of several cases where the information was withheld, only to surface after the marriage. It has always resulted in disaster.

The lesson to be taken from this is that a husband and wife must have complete trust in each other. Trust is the single most important component of a successful marriage. *Never do anything that might jeopardize your wife's trust in you.*

As noted above, you have never had a wife before. You have no idea of what any wife in general expects, and you don't know what your wife in particular will expect of you. She may have expectations based on what she has seen of her parents' interactions. For example, she may become upset if you do not ask whether she needs a new dress for her cousin's upcoming wedding. She may point out that her father always would ask her mother whether she needed a new dress for a wedding. Of course, when she remembers her father's asking this, her parents had already been married for a number of years. Her father also probably did not know to ask this question three months after he was married. You might say, "My dear wife, I'm not good at guessing. Eventually I will learn, but please, when you want something, tell me. It's the only way I can know."

Speaking of clothing, let me mention what the *Menoras HaMaor* says (*Ner* 3): "Economize on your own clothes. Clothe your children according to your means, but extend yourself beyond your means for your wife's clothing."

You should realize that women are physiologically different from men. They have hormonal changes that men do not experience. Some women may have fluctuating moods due to these hormonal changes. They may be irritable, become angry, or cry for no apparent reason. After a few days this moodiness disappears and they are as pleasant and jolly as ever. If this cycle is not understood, a husband may be bewildered and the wife may be desperate. They may each think something is seriously wrong. They may place blame rather than realize that such mood changes are not uncommon and can be managed fairly easily if properly understood. In preparation for marriage, I suggest you read my book, *Getting Up When You're Down*.[1] It can eliminate unnecessary friction.

You should know that your wife is your wife — not your mother. She does not have to behave as if she were your mother. Your mother may have catered to you, having raised you from infancy. Don't expect this of your wife.

You will likely have different taste in foods. You may love gefilte fish, but she can't abide it. Perhaps at her parents' home they began the Shabbos-day meal with chopped liver, while you are accustomed to fish at that *seudah*. I trust that you are far too intelligent to make an issue of such trivia.

Your mother may have been a meticulous housekeeper. As they say, "You could eat off the floor." Even if your wife's mother held herself to the same standard, your wife may not have or, more likely, *cannot* rise to the same level of cleanliness. Years ago, the housewife (her mother, or perhaps even her grandmother) was just that. It was rare for a young married woman to hold down a job (even part-time). Nowadays, much of the burden of *parnassah* (livelihood) falls on the

1. *Getting Up When You're Down: A Mature Discussion of an Adult Malady —
Depression and Related Conditions* (Shaar Press, 1997).

wife. She is very likely overburdened with all her new obligations. Even if she held the same job prior to her marriage, at that point she came home to a clean house, fresh laundry, and an appetizing meal, all prepared by someone else. These responsibilities are now hers. If a "spotless" home is not her top priority, it is likely that she is prioritizing wisely. If Hashem blesses you early in your marriage and your wife is expecting (even if she does not suffer from morning sickness), that is another factor that moves efficient housekeeping one further notch down on the must-do list. Learn to look at the big picture: you are married to this wonderful young lady and together you will build a *bayis ne'eman*. Nowhere in the Torah is *bayis ne'eman* translated as "an immaculate home." If some aspect of your beloved spouse's housekeeping skills falls short of the standard you so admire, roll up your sleeves and pitch in. And don't act as if you are doing her a favor; you are simply doing your share. Don't act as if you are a martyr if you wash the floor or put away the dishes; you don't expect her to feel that way, do you? Just do your part and you will find it helps keep your *shalom bayis* (marital harmony) intact. You will be better for it, your wife will appreciate it, and your new home will be both blessed *and* clean.

One newlywed young man complained to his Rosh Yeshivah that his wife was not a good *balebusta* (housekeeper). The following day he answered the door and was surprised to see his esteemed Rosh Yeshivah, who came into the apartment, found the broom, dustpan, and mop, and showed the young man how to clean up.

By the way, there is a tradition that one should do something to help prepare for Shabbos. (That is in addition to mopping the floor.)

A young man consulted the Steipler Gaon about a difficult gemara. As the young man was about to leave, the Steipler said, "Young man, I see that you are a masmid (diligent student). Don't forget to help your wife at home."

The young man said, "My wife is a true eishes chayil (woman of valor). Her greatest wish is that I learn Torah."

The Steipler nodded. "Yes," he said, "that is her mitzvah. Your mitzvah is to help at home."

Hashem will bless you with children. Infants usually awaken several times during the night. You enjoy your sleep and hate being woken. Furthermore, you may think, *I can't feed the baby, so what point is there in getting out of bed?*

Gestation and childbirth are indeed normal conditions, but they are a drain on a woman's energy. After childbirth, a mother needs much rest (another reason to read *Getting Up When You're Down*). When you hear the baby cry during the night, get up, diaper the baby, and give the child to your wife to feed. When the feeding is over, the baby needs to be burped. Let your wife go back to sleep; you burp the baby.

"But," you may protest, "I need my sleep. If I get up to the baby I will not be able to concentrate well on my learning tomorrow." I suspect that this is the rationalization of the *yetzer hara* (evil inclination) rather than the counsel of the *yetzer tov* (good inclination).

You can become a *gaon* by burping the baby! Your uncles were born when I was in medical school. During the night, I would put a medical text on the dresser and read while I burped and rocked the baby. This was an excellent time for study, and I am certain this enabled me to graduate with honors! Don't lose this opportunity. Stand a *sefer* on the dresser. You will learn much and have a healthy, well-rested wife.

> *The Alter Rebbe of Lubavitch lived in an apartment above that of his son, the Mittler Rebbe. One time the Alter Rebbe heard an infant crying incessantly. He went down and found the Mittler Rebbe so engrossed in Torah study that he did not hear the baby's cry. The Alter Rebbe sharply rebuked his son. As great as Torah study is, it should never make one oblivious to a child's cry.*

Your in-laws will come to visit. Halachah requires that you respect them. Incidentally, there are far too many jokes about mothers-in-law. Don't tell them to your wife. Those jokes are not funny nor are they cute. You would not want to hear such comments about your own mother (who is also a mother-in-law, by the way).

One of the vexing problems today is whether a woman should work, pursue a career, or be a homemaker — or all three. Western civilization has been influenced by the feminist movement. There are many things about this movement that are valid. For example, there is no reason why a woman should be paid less than a man is for a similar job. However, other elements are not so clear. Some have the attitude that unless a woman has a professional or business career, she has an inferior position in society.

You can't build walls against attitudes. Some young women who were taught Torah *hashkafos* (outlooks) in seminary may nevertheless envy the woman who has become a lawyer or CEO of a major firm. Furthermore, there are men who secretly — or not so secretly — admire a woman who has achieved such an accomplishment. The woman who has five children, three of them in diapers, may have a feeling of missing out on success in life, and possibly even of oppression. She may feel she has little to show for herself if at the end of the day she is totally exhausted and is confronted by a huge pile of laundry and a sink full of dirty dishes.

Granted, it is often necessary for a wife to work. It is also a common practice that the wife may be helping support the husband who is learning in *kollel*. She may be happy to do so, because she has been taught and sincerely believes that this is her *tafkid* (purpose). She gladly works and does her utmost to care for the children and the household. All this notwithstanding, she is only human, and is subject to viewing with some envy the professional woman whose life seems to be so much more glamorous and less stressful. And if your wife is indeed a career woman, balancing home, children, spouse, and work, she may be even more overwhelmed by all her responsibilities.

Rabbi Akiva gave his wife, Rachel, a gold necklace and pendant of Jerusalem. He said, "She truly deserves this. She sacrificed so much for Torah." You must take every opportunity to acknowledge your appreciation of your wife's efforts. This does not necessarily mean that you should spend an exorbitant sum on jewelry when the total household income barely allows you to make ends meet. Rather, small tokens of appreciation, presented with a warm, admiring smile, will doubtless be valued as much as diamonds.

In addition to according her the respect that is her due, there is another aspect to your open appreciation of your wife: Your children will learn from you to respect their mother. Just as parents have an obligation to give proper *chinuch* (training) to their children in all other mitzvos, they are equally obligated to give them *chinuch* in respect for their parents. This is accomplished not by lecturing, but by modeling. They will respect their mother if you respect her.

You may get enjoyment in teasing. There is a proverb, " *Wer es liebt sich, necht sich*, Where love is present, teasing is present." My advice to you: *Don't tease!* There are much better ways of expressing affection. What you may think is clever and cute might be felt by your wife as a sharp sting. Stinging remarks are not easily forgotten.

There are some men who are domineering and give orders to their wives as though the men were five-star generals. They justify their behavior by quoting a statement that is indeed cited in halachah: A proper woman is one who does the will of her husband (*Tanna D'Vei Eliyahu* 9:8).

Our Sages are very critical of people who distort Torah for their own purposes. What if the husband wanted her to cook something for him on Shabbos? Is she to do his will in order to be a "proper wife"? In order to understand what this statement means, we must know its origin.

Scripture gives an account of a battle between the armies of Sisera and Israel (*Judges* 4:17-21). Sisera's forces were defeated and he fled, finding asylum in the tent of Yael, a Kenite woman. Yael knew that her husband had a peace agreement with Sisera. However, she realized that Sisera was a threat to Israel, and she also knew that her husband valued Israel above Sisera. When Sisera fell asleep in her tent, she killed him. She had correctly interpreted her husband's will. The Sages, therefore, cite her as an example of a woman who understands what her husband would want her to do under certain circumstances.

How this can be distorted to give a husband dictatorial rights is beyond me. There is no justification for tyrannical behavior.

I observed my parents' marriage for 43 years. There was profound mutual respect, consideration, and love. As you know, Zeide first met Bobbe *at* the wedding ceremony. Their marriage was not based on "fish-love." The stresses they went through early in their marriage would have destroyed a "fish-love" relationship. The only complaint I remember Bobbe having is that after 50 years of married life she still did not know what foods Zeide preferred, since he ate whatever she prepared. To have shown a preference would have meant that she might have to go out of her way or do extra work. Preventing Bobbe from extending herself beyond reasonable bounds was far more important to him than requesting any particular food.

You know that when Zeide found out that he had pancreatic cancer, he took it right in stride. Zeide knew a great deal about medicine, and was correct in his assessment that chemotherapy for this form of cancer was not effective. He said to me, "If it could prolong my life, I would have to accept the unpleasant side effects. But to suffer for no purpose makes no sense." I agreed that there was no point in chemotherapy.

The doctor who spoke to Bobbe told her that the most that could be expected from chemotherapy was another three months of life. Bobbe said, "Three months? Why, to extend his life for even three days you would have to do it."

Zeide said to me, "I'm sorry the doctor gave Bobbe false hope. But if I do not take the chemotherapy, then when I die, Bobbe will say, 'Why didn't I insist on it? He might still be alive!' Bobbe will then feel guilty, and I wouldn't want that. So I will take the chemotherapy with all its miseries. I've done many things for Bobbe. This gives me a chance to do the last thing I can for her."

Indeed, theirs was not "fish-love."

There is a natural tendency to blame others. That's how mankind got into trouble right at the beginning. When G-d asked Adam if he had eaten from the forbidden fruit, his response was, "My wife made me do it." Eve, in turn, blamed the serpent. Neither of them took responsibility for their actions. Perhaps if Adam had just said, "I did wrong and I regret it," he would have been forgiven and the course of world history would have been much different.

Rashi points out how strong the urge to divest oneself of responsibility can be. The matriarch Rachel was desperate to have children, so much so that she said, "Give me children — otherwise I am dead" (*Genesis* 30:1). The Midrash says that when Joseph was born and her fondest wish was realized, she said, "Now if something breaks I will have someone to blame it on. I can say that the baby did it" (*Rashi*, ibid. 30:23).[1] Think of it! Is it possible to imagine that in her moment of supreme joy, when she felt that she finally had a reason to live,

1. *Bereishis* 30:23 records that when Rachel gave birth to Joseph she explained: "G-d has taken away [*asaf*] my disgrace." The Rabbis observe that until a woman gives birth, whatever blame [there is, within the house] is placed upon her. If she breaks a vessel within the house, whom shall she blame for this? Once she has given birth, she places the blame on her child (*Tanchuma, Vayeitzei* 19).

our mother Rachel was happy because she will now have someone to blame for a dish being broken? It seems to me that the Midrash tells us this only to impress upon us the intensity of the urge to place blame on someone else.

The reason the Torah relates this about Adam and about Rachel is to alert us to the proclivity of people to blame others. Be on guard against this human frailty.

Why is this tendency to blame others so strong? It is because if we can blame others then we do not feel we have to make any changes in ourselves. *It's the other person's fault. Let her/him change. I'm fine the way I am.* We are set in our ways and we do not like to change. Blaming others allows us to stay the way we are. This is as natural a response as reflexively putting your hand in front of your face to protect yourself from a flying object. You must catch yourself and make a concerted effort to avoid blaming. But I can assure you that in any instance where something is not to your liking, if you succeed in refraining from blaming, it will be a major contribution to a happy marriage.

The Talmud says that when a man and woman are united in marriage, Hashem's Presence dwells with them (*Sotah* 17a). That is, if you let Him.

> *When the Rebbe of Kotzk was a young man, R' Simchah Bunim of P'shische asked him, "Young man, where is G-d?"*
>
> *"There is no place where He is not present," the young R' Mendel answered.*
>
> *"Young man, I asked you, 'Where is G-d?'" R' Simchah Bunim repeated.*

"The whole world is filled with His glory," R' Mendel answered.

Again R' Simchah Bunim said, "Young man, I have asked you, 'Where is G-d?'"

R' Mendel said, "If my answers do not satisfy you, then please tell me."

R' Simchah Bunim said, "G-d is present wherever He is invited to be."

Yes, G-d is everywhere, but we can cause Him to withdraw His Presence.

There are essentially two human traits that repel Hashem. One is *ga'avah*. Hashem says, "A vain person and I cannot dwell in the same abode" (*Sotah* 5a). Earlier I pointed out the grievous error of men considering women to be inferior. If a husband has an attitude of superiority, which is generally manifested by his being demanding, domineering, and inconsiderate of his wife, he drives Hashem away. My dear grandson, I regret to tell you that I know of homes where all the mitzvos seemingly are meticulously observed, but it is a home devoid of Hashem's Presence because someone there is a *baal ga'avah*.

As we well know, Hashem is repelled by idolatry. Of course, there will never be any idols in your home. That is just unthinkable. Statuary idols, that is. But flying into a rage is equivalent to idolatry (*Rambam, Hilchos Dei'os* 2). I can understand that you may feel anger, especially in a situation where you feel you have been provoked, but you must exercise great restraint not to erupt into a rage. If you lose your temper, it is equivalent to removing all the *mezuzos* from your doors. Hashem does not wish to be in a place where there is idol worship. That is precisely what happens when a person loses control of his anger.

Earlier I quoted the Torah's description of the marriage relationship, "They shall be as one flesh." Husband and wife should be one. Now if you injured your foot, would you become angry at it for causing you pain? Would you hit your foot? A Torah-observant person fulfills the Torah's concept of marriage. It should be as absurd to be angry at your wife as at any other part of you. You may feel hurt, but not angry.

You may say, "Zeide, what is it that you are expecting of me? I am not an angel!"

Some people think that it is beyond human capacity to observe Shabbos appropriately, or to avoid any foods that may contain a trace of something non-kosher. They may say, "How can you expect me to make a living if I refuse to work on Shabbos?" Or, "Shabbos is the only time I can visit my friends, do my chores, or make necessary contacts. I cannot possibly avoid traveling or using the telephone." Or someone may say, "My work requires me to travel all over the country all week. I cannot possibly adhere to strict *kashrus*. What do you want me to do, starve? I am a human being, not an angel."

It is only a matter of degree. One does not have to be an angel to observe Shabbos and *kashrus*, and one does not have to be an angel to control one's temper. Nor does one have to be an angel to think of his wife as part of himself and act accordingly. Zeide was not an angel. He was a great person, a superb human being. And by the way, that is better than being an angel.

Although achieving control over anger may be difficult, you can get a great assist from *Iggeres HaRamban*, the Ramban's *Letter to His*

Son. Not only does it contain excellent instructions, but the Ramban also says that on the day one reads it, his prayers will be answered. Of course, the Ramban is not referring to prayers for winning the lottery, but to prayers for greater spirituality. Ramban suggests you read this letter once a week. I recommend that you make a fixed time each week to read it.

The Talmud is very harsh with a husband who terrorizes his household. "Whoever exercises excessive fear over his household will eventually come to transgress the three sins: forbidden relations, bloodshed, and violation of Shabbos" (*Gittin* 6b). If the family is running late with their Shabbos preparations on Friday afternoon, the instructions to get ready must be said in a soft, pleasant tone (*Shabbos* 34a).

> *R' Z'eira lived to an old age. When his students asked by what merit he achieved his longevity, he said, "I never showed anger in my house" (Megillah 28a).*

Speaking in a soft and gentle voice contributes to everyone's longevity.

While there is some controversy about what portions of Torah women should study, there is universal agreement that they should learn about the mitzvos that are incumbent upon them. This includes not only the laws of Shabbos but also the mitzvah of *emunah* (faith in Hashem) and all the *middos* required by the Torah. I suggest that you have a *shiur* with your wife, studying *sefarim* such as *Mesillas Yesharim* and *Chovos HaLevavos* (*Duties of the Heart*). Learning together creates a strong bond.

I advise that you and your wife begin to prepare yourself for being parents by reading books on parenting. We don't come into the world as accomplished doctors, lawyers, or electricians. Much study is necessary to acquire these skills. There is no reason to assume that we are born with the ability to be competent parents.

Unless there is adequate preparation for parenting, parents may have divergent ideas about raising children. This can cause much confusion for the child. The time to decide on a course that both parents agree on is *before* the children are born. There is one caveat to this: We can never know what life will bring and how many unexpected challenges we will have to face. A plan is only as good as our ability to revise it when necessary. Parenting cannot be so rigid that "this" is the way it has to be. Children are not "one size fits all," and parenting must adapt to the needs of each child. Flexibility must go hand in hand with *chinuch* to be effective.

The commentaries on *tefillah* ask why it is necessary to verbalize our prayers. Inasmuch as Hashem knows our innermost thoughts, why do we simply not meditate? What is gained by actively pronouncing the words?

Various answers have been given. I am bold enough to suggest an additional answer.

There appears to be an inner resistance to acknowledging gratitude. As we mentioned earlier, the first human being, Adam, was an ingrate (*Rashi, Genesis* 3:12). The best gift he ever received was his wife, Eve. Nonetheless, when G-d questioned him regarding having eaten from the Tree of Knowledge, Adam's initial response was, "Don't blame me. The woman *You* gave me caused the whole mess."

Similarly, Moses sharply rebuked the Israelites for being ingrates. This reluctance to acknowledge a kindness can be seen even in small children. Mother may say, "Now say 'thank you' to the nice man for the candy," and the child's grunt indicates that he has no intention of complying.

Tosafos (*Avodah Zarah* 5a) state that the reason the Israelites did not want to acknowledge their gratitude to Hashem is because they did not want to feel beholden to Him. This is a profound psychological insight. When we have strong negative feelings about an issue, our minds may render us oblivious to it. Even small children may react this way.

It is even more difficult to feel obligated and beholden to another human being than it is to Hashem. We may find it easier to express our gratitude to Hashem. If we do so frequently, and if we accustom ourselves to pronounce the words "I thank You" to Hashem, we may lessen our resistance to saying them to another person. This is one advantage of verbalizing our prayers.

When we declare our love to Hashem in prayer, we realize that although Hashem knows we love Him, we express it verbally anyway. That is a good precedent. We should apply it to the people we love.

In *tefillah* we confess our sins. We express our regret for having done wrong and pledge not to repeat our sins. In human interaction, admitting one was wrong is greatly resisted. People often rationalize and justify their actions, and they may obstinately refuse to admit they were wrong. When we say to Hashem, "I have sinned and I ask Your forgiveness," we may reduce our resistance to saying this to other people.

My dear grandson, if there is any formula for a successful marriage, it is to utilize these expressions when they are called for. The three short phrases, "I thank you," "I love you," and "I am sorry; I was wrong," are "magic charms" for making your marriage a happy one.

As was noted earlier, true love for another person is an unselfish love. A beautiful chassidic story illustrates this point:

The *tzaddik*, R' Moshe Leib of Sassov, has come down in chassidic lore as unparalleled in *ahavas Yisrael*. R' Moshe Leib said that he learned what *ahavah* means from a drunkard.

> *While passing a tavern, R' Moshe Leib overheard a conversation between two inebriated men. "I love you, Stefan," the first one said.*
>
> *"You just say that, Ivan," Stefan responded. "You don't really love me." The two kept on exchanging these assertions until Stefan finally said, "If you really love me, Ivan, then tell me — where am I hurting?"*
>
> *R' Moshe Leib said, "Ahavas Yisrael means knowing other people's pain without them telling you where it hurts."*

This is the kind of love that should develop between husband and wife. Just as one knows one's own needs, wants, and pain, so one should know that of the spouse. I don't expect this to occur at the very beginning of the relationship. However, it will develop if you make a concerted effort to develop it.

My dear grandson, be extremely cautious about your words. I think that the reason our Sages formulated this prayer with the words, "*Baruch She'amar vehayah ha'olam*, Blessed is He **Who spoke** and the world came into being," instead of "*Baruch Borei ha'olam*, Blessed is the **Creator** of the world," is because they wished to stress that the spoken word can create an entire world. By the same token, a spoken word can destroy a world. The prophet says, "Their tongue is like a drawn arrow" (*Jeremiah* 9:7). Actually, the tongue is even more powerful than an arrow. A suit of armor can repel an arrow. Sharp words can pierce the strongest armor. Some of the wisest words spoken by a human being are those in the Ramban's *Letter to His Son*: "Think about what you wish to say before you say it." I cannot begin to tell you how much misery would have been avoided if people had followed the Ramban's advice.

My dear grandson, do not make non-issues into issues. I received a call from a husband who was very frustrated with his wife because she does not tighten the lid on jars. "When I pick up the jar, the lid comes off in my hand and the jar falls to the floor," he said.

I answered, "Don't pick up a jar by the lid." It seemed to me that he was looking for something to be an issue.

In the best of relationships unforeseen problems may arise. It is extremely important to nip these in the bud. Unresolved problems tend to not go away. To the contrary, they may become more complicated with time.

It is indeed important to have a *chaver* in whom you can confide. However, if any problem arises in the relationship, *physical or emotional,* do not ask your peers for advice; their advice is undoubtedly tinged by their own relationship with their spouses. Seek the advice of wisdom and experience. Discuss all issues with a mentor who has the benefit of age and training (i.e., a rabbi or a psychologist). Their prudence, sagacity, and rational discernment will guide you in the right direction.

The last person with whom to discuss any "problem" in your marriage is a parent. Long after the problem has been resolved and you and your wife have forgotten all about it, your parent may unwittingly harbor a degree of resentment against your spouse for having caused you to suffer.

When I say "last," I mean it two ways. After you have exhausted all other options, if a problem persists or is not solvable (i.e., abuse — either physical or emotional), do tell your parents so they can support you in your decisions.

You will remember that when Solomon died and Rehoboam ascended the throne, he was confronted by the populace that wanted the taxation to be eased. The elders counseled Rehoboam to be flexible and respect the complaints of the populace. Rehoboam's peers advised him to take a hard line and assert his authority. Rehoboam favored the advice of his peers over the counsel of his elders, precipitating a catastrophic partition of the nation of Israel from which we have never recovered.

As noted, when you need advice to resolve a marital issue, consult an older person who is wise and experienced in couples counseling. Of course, age in itself is no guarantee of wisdom, but you can certainly find a person whose maturity and clarity of thought make him a resource for advice. If necessary, do not hesitate to seek the advice of a professional counselor.

I can testify that, as a psychiatrist, I have been consulted by people with serious marital problems. In many instances these problems could have been avoided had they been dealt with at the onset, when their resolution was relatively simple. These couples did not seek professional help earlier, either because they believed they could work it out themselves or more often, because they felt embarrassed to do so. There is still a widespread attitude that there is a stigma attached to consulting a professional counselor, and people may seek help only when the problem has reached desperate proportions. Do not be so foolish.

People who detect a minor problem with their automobile are likely to consult a mechanic promptly. They generally do not consult their friends, and they certainly do not wait until the car breaks down before asking for competent help.

We are not born mechanics. It takes study and experience to develop those skills. Neither are we born as competent spouses or parents. Being a spouse or parent is a huge responsibility, and we should realize that we need education and training to achieve competence.

This brings me to the next item. One of the great mysteries is why Hashem arranged it so that people have their greatest wisdom when they need it least. By the time a person reaches retirement age, life has taught him a great deal. However, at this point he does not need to make any major decisions. The really important decisions — whom to marry, what career to choose, where to live, how to raise one's children — have all been made when we were young and inexperienced. Why shouldn't we have our maximum wisdom between ages 18 and 30, when we need it most?

I can only conclude that in His infinite wisdom, Hashem knows that maximum energy and maximum wisdom do not go together. When we are young, we have our maximum energy, but our wisdom is at its lowest. When we are old, we have our maximum wisdom, but our energy is at its lowest.

What is the solution? It is that energetic youth should avail itself of the wisdom of the elders. That is the best of all possible worlds. Unfortunately, many young people are headstrong and think they know it all. This can result in tragic consequences.

So be wise, and apply your great energies guided by the wisdom of experience.

You and your wife should read books on parenting that have a *frum hashkafah* (religious perspective) and then discuss the various issues and decide how you will optimally resolve them in your own home. You may choose *Positive Parenting*[1] as a starter. This book was written with the collaboration of one of the finest child psychologists in the country. Reading it will give you and your wife an opportunity to have a unified and consistent approach in parenting.

Young children are exceedingly canny. They know how to play one parent against the other. Proper preparation can help you avoid this problem.

No doubt your mother and I made some mistakes in raising our children, and your parents no doubt made their mistakes. You, too, are entitled to make mistakes, but temper them with love and you and your children will be able to develop positive relationships.

Children need both love and discipline. These two elements may sometimes appear to be in conflict, but with a proper foundation, discipline can be seen as a form of love. However, it must be discipline that is directed toward the child's betterment rather than a result of parents' anger or frustration. Uneducated parents may vacillate between lenience and firmness. There is nothing as confusing to children as the inconsistencies of their parents.

1. *Positive Parenting: Developing Your Child's Potential,* with Dr. Ursula Verena Schwartz (ArtScroll / Mesorah Publications, 1996).

Preparing yourselves before the children come onto the scene is most advantageous. An ounce of prevention is worth a pound of cure, as the old saying avers. Once problems arise, you are in a state of stress, which may result in knee-jerk reactions. Discussing in advance how you and your wife plan to respond to issues that may arise can prevent many problems so long as you both are in agreement as to how to proceed and realize that your decisions may have to be revised depending on individual circumstances.

My dear grandson, with Hashem's blessing, you will be bringing children into this world. Your relationship to your children will derive from the inborn love of a parent for a child. Children are brought into this difficult world and they have no say in that decision. Parents, therefore, have an obligation to provide their children with the best means to adjust to this world. Their motivation should be to do what is best for their children. The children should not be expected to satisfy the parents' emotional needs.

Very often parents make decisions based on what they believe others may think of them. In order to stroke their own egos and be perceived as having the "best" kids, they push their children into schools and camps that may not be in the child's best interest. They may dress their children in designer clothing in order to impress their neighbors and friends, and they may purchase the latest toys or games simply because they are status symbols. These types of behavior are detrimental to the psychological growth of children.

Being a parent is a major responsibility. Yes, it's true that parents are not infallible, but if the parents' primary goal is to do the best for their child(ren) in the best way they see fit, then with the help of Hashem, the "third Partner" in childrearing, they will succeed. In this

— 181 —

vein, it is important to note that heartfelt *tefillos* — including a mother's tears — are the most effective weapon we have in our arsenal.

Your children will respect and honor you as the Torah commands. It is important, however, that they know that you consider yourself valuable to them as a parent. Some parents spend so much time at work that they do not have much time to spend with their children. They may say, "I have to spend this time at work so that I can provide the children with all their needs."

Yes, children indeed have many needs that require money. However, they also have a great need for closeness with their parents. Giving them *things* instead of *yourself* is making a statement that you consider the things you give them as being of greater value than yourself. If parents so degrade themselves, it is little wonder that the children's respect for them may suffer.

Giving respect to parents is not optional. It does not depend on whether or not that parent was good at parenting, and children must understand this. Even if your mother and your father fall short of your expectations, you still must respect and honor them. It is obvious that this mitzvah is much easier to fulfill when the parents give honor and respect to their children; this aspect is not a Torah commandment. However, *Ethics of the Fathers* 4:1 states, "Who is deserving of honor? The one who honors others." Children are included under the blanket term *others*. Make it easier for them to do the mitzvah. After all, the reward for *kibbud av v'eim* is *arichas yamim* — a long life. There is no parent who does not want a long life for his/her children. One who is given honor, respect, and love will reciprocate in kind.

Self-respect, respect for others, and being respected by others go hand in hand. If you give of yourself to your children, you are making a statement that you have self-respect, and this encourages them to respect you.

I mentioned the fact that the Rambam places the duties of the husband toward his wife before those of the wife to her husband, and that this should teach us who must initiate respect for the other. There is another nuance in this Rambam that is often overlooked.

Rambam says that "a husband should respect his wife more than himself and love her as he loves himself" (*Hilchos Ishus* 15:19). The origin of this halachah is the Gemara cited earlier, that "one should love his wife as much as he loves himself, and respect her even *more* than he respects himself" (*Yevamos* 62b). Why does Rambam reverse the order of the Gemara, placing respect *before* love?

I believe that the reason is that to love one's wife as much as one loves himself is unlikely to be achieved from the first moment of marriage. A strong love develops gradually. However, *respect must begin from the very first moment.*

I am sure that by following these teachings of Rambam and by developing your *middos*, you and your dear *kallah* will have a blissful marriage to 120 years.

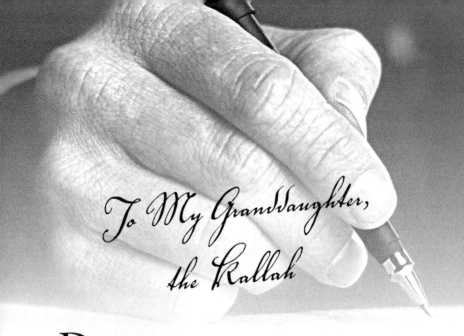

To My Granddaughter, the Kallah

Dear Granddaughter:

When your cousin became a *chassan*, I shared with him some thoughts that I feel are important in marriage. Please read the above letter, "To My Grandson, the *Chassan*." Much of what I wrote there can apply to you, as a *kallah*, as well, but there are some points I wish to mention that are not included there. Your *chassan* should read this letter, too.

Baruch Hashem, your *chassan* is a fine *ben Torah*, and from what I hear, has exemplary *middos*. He comes from a *chashuvah mishpachah*, and I am sure that Hashem will bless your marriage to be a *binyan adei ad*, and that you will be a source of much *nachas* to your *mishpachos*.

The Steipler Gaon, reacting to a request for advice about some adjustment problems early in a marriage, said, "What do you expect? For the past twelve years this young man had no relationship with anything except his *shtender.*"

This is a new relationship for both of you, like nothing you have ever experienced before. You both need to acknowledge this, have a great deal of patience, and be willing to give each other much consideration and understanding. There are things that may be important to you but of which he has no idea. For example, as I noted in the letter to your cousin, it is possible that in your family, no significance was accorded to a birthday, whereas in his family it was an important event. You have to give each other time to learn what is important to each of you.

Each family has different *minhagim.* Each one should respect the other family's *minhagim.* On *Yamim Tovim,* families have their own *minhagim,* especially on Pesach. You've been accustomed to your father's Seder and to the *nigunim* with which he recites the Haggadah; having a different type of Seder may make you feel uncomfortable. I have heard of young women who broke down in tears at their in-laws' Seder. Give yourself time. All *minhagim* have a source in *kedushah,* but her unfamiliarity with different practices may cause a young woman to feel that she has been torn from her home base.

Some *minhagim* may verge on halachah. For example, people who do not eat *gebrokts* may see this as a halachah rather than a *minhag.* A Rav can be consulted to clarify what is a halachah and what is a *minhag.* Although *minhagim* are important, they should not become issues impacting your *shalom bayis.* Generally speaking, a wife takes on her husband's *minhagim,* but certainly compromises and adjustments should be open for discussion.

Don't jump to conclusions. If your husband wants to spend time with his *chavrusa*, don't misinterpret this to mean that he does not value your companionship. You have a right to spend time with your friends, and so does he. This is not an indication that one does not value the company of the spouse.

Be open about making your needs and desires known to him. He is not a mind reader. Don't assume that he should know what you want. Tell him. Don't hint. He may not be good at guessing.

Realize that up to now you have had a twenty-year relationship with your father, and you have come to love and respect him a great deal. Do not compare your husband to your father. When you marry, you accept your husband's *minhagim* and you should be proud to follow his lead. To cite a minor example, just because your father says a *dvar Torah* at the beginning of the Shabbos *seudah* does not mean that your husband is wrong when he presents *his dvar Torah* just before *bentching*. Your father and your husband should each be accepted and loved, not critically compared.

Understand that your husband, too, had a long-standing relationship with his father and may hold him in high esteem. He may not wish to act differently from his father's example. If you have a problem with his actions, your husband is caught between disappointing you and disappointing his father. You and your husband should have an amicable discussion in which you come to a mutual decision regarding *minhagim* and *chumros*. However, as noted, remember that a wife is generally expected to follow her husband's customs. He will most likely intend to follow his own father's *minhagim*, as he grew up with them, and a good wife will follow her husband in these matters.

Yet sometimes it is important to consult parents for guidance. They have had much experience in life. When we're young, we tend to think we know it all. Sure, you may be much handier programming an electronic device than your parents are, but they are still much wiser than you. Listen to their suggestions and give them proper consideration, but ultimately your decisions should be those arrived at by you and your husband.

Your parents remember you as a tiny, helpless infant. They had to decide everything for you. It is only for perhaps the past several years that they began to see you as being capable of making decisions. They still may have the urge to protect you, and it may be hard for them to realize that you are a mature adult. Nevertheless, if you and your husband are mature enough to marry, you should be mature enough to make your own decisions as a couple.

My father was fanatical about his children's health. When I had a cold, he would call to make sure that we had called the doctor, that I was drinking enough hot tea, and that I was warmly dressed. My wife took offense at this. "Doesn't he think I know how to take care of you?" As time passed, she came to understand his great concern about our health, and did not feel offended.

You and your husband are a unit and should function as such. Do not delegate talking to parents to your spouse; for example, by saying, "You talk to my father about it. I'm not comfortable doing so." Whatever issues arise, discuss them with your parents together.

A most important decision you will have to make is what type of life you plan to lead. Some young men spend several years in *kollel*, and then make earning a livelihood their primary focus. Others choose to be lifelong scholars. This is a decision that only you and your husband can make. This cannot be decided by your parents, rebbeim, friends, or community. You may listen to all of them, but the ultimate decision must be yours. You cannot live your lives by what other people want.

Parents often support a young couple. This is done out of love. Supporting children does not justify controlling them. You must realize that when parents supply full support, they often wish to have more of a say in what their children do and how they spend the money. If you are expecting to receive full support, you should also expect to experience more hands-on interactions with your parents and in-laws.

On this topic, it often happens that the in-laws may wish to participate in their children's lives by offering tangible evidence of their love as well as monetary gifts. For example, one mother might feel that sending fresh-baked challah to her married children is a sign that she loves them and is thinking about them every time she bakes. If you would love to bake your own challah and therefore do not appreciate this gift, tension may arise where there is no need for it. Accept her bounty and serve her challah as well as your own, knowing that she has baked for you out of love, not out of a wish to control you. Perhaps you can gently hint that you prefer to bake your own challah and ask for her recipe. Be generous with your compliments and voice your *hakaras hatov* for her gesture. Eventually a satisfactory solution will be worked out; in this way you will both be able to fulfill your needs.

Regardless of how you look at it, marriage means detachment from parents. Someone else has now become the most important person in your life. Loving a spouse does not detract from the love of one's parents, but, logistically, one cannot spend the same amount of time with one's parents as one did in the past. Be sensitive to your parents' feelings. Keep in contact with them, certainly by phone, and whenever it is convenient, visit them in person. They still have much wisdom to offer you, if you are wise enough to see it. My own ego prevented me from realizing this for some time, as the following incident shows.

After I became a Rav, I was scheduled to deliver a eulogy and my father asked, "What do you plan to say?" This irritated me. I felt, *If you don't trust me to speak well, don't put me in the position of giving the eulogy.* Much later I realized how foolish I had been. My father had offered to guide me, but I rejected his assistance. Parents want to help, but as impetuous young people, we may resent their assistance, even when we need it. We should be wise enough to accept it.

Both sets of parents may claim your attention. They both love you, and when you have children, they both want the *nachas* of their grandchildren. You can't be with both of them at the same time, but don't make calculations: "We've spent four Shabbosim with your parents and only two with mine." Your time is not a pie that needs to be divided exactly in half. At times you might prefer to have a private Shabbos by yourself, which is reasonable, but remember, there are couples who wish that they still had parents to visit.

I was many times a grandfather when my mother died. I did not need her to do my laundry or make my lunches. But when I could no longer call her to tell her about a new baby or about something clever one of the children said, I missed her. Value your parents as long as Hashem allows you to have them.

With Hashem's blessing, you will have children. Disputes sometimes erupt when each set of parents wants the child to be named after someone in his/her family or when someone wants you to give a name to which you have an intense aversion. The *sefarim* say that Hashem inspires the baby's parents with which name to give. You may consult your parents, but the decision should be your husband's and yours. However, a sign of maturity is the ability to try to please others. Don't reject a suggestion out of hand — a cute young child with an uncommon name can be twice as cute. I can assure that nothing is so important that it should create a rift between you and your in-laws or, *chas v'shalom*, between you and your spouse.

It is only natural that in marriage some disagreements may occur. Make every effort to resolve these quickly, and if you need help in doing so, do not hesitate to ask for it. There will be times when you wish to apprise your spouse of behavior that you find offensive or beneath him. Do so gently, with respect and consideration. You may criticize the act, but not the person.

Some people think that raising one's voice accentuates one's point. The fact is that just the opposite is true. When you raise your voice, the other person tunes you out. Instead of listening to what you're saying, he is thinking of how to respond. King Solomon writes, "The gentle words of the wise are heard" (*Ecclesiastes* 9:17). As noted above, the Talmud says that R' Z'eira attributed his long life to the fact that he never raised his voice.

A preacher left the text of his sermon on the lectern. Someone saw that he had made comments in the margin, like "Pause,"

"Go soft and slow." At one point he had written, "Argument awfully weak here. Yell loudly!"

If your argument has merit, it will be received best if you speak softly.

When criticizing the act, address the particular incident. Do not say "You never …," or "You always …," even if it is something that occurs repeatedly.

Accept constructive criticism with gratitude. "Admonish a wise man and he will love you" (*Proverbs* 9:8). "Listen to advice and accept reprimand, that you may grow wise in the end" (ibid., 19:20). When is criticism constructive? When it is given out of a sincere desire to help the person and you are willing to help him/her make any necessary changes. If you are angry, postpone the criticism until the anger has passed and you are in a mellower mood. If you criticize when you are angry, you are very likely to regret it later.

It has been noted that men and women tend to react differently. A woman may cry when angry, and it may seem that she is sad. On the other hand, when a man is sad, he may express anger rather than show his sadness. Give yourselves time to learn what your spouse's responses indicate.

Do not carry resentments. Forgive quickly. Sometimes a spouse may resurrect something that happened twenty years ago. King Solomon writes, "Anger rests in the bosom of fools" (*Ecclesiastes* 7:9). Hanging on to resentment is utter folly. I dealt with this at length in my book, *Forgiveness*.[1]

Husbands and wives should not try to control each other. If there

---

1. *Forgiveness: Don't Let Resentment Keep You Captive* (Shaar Press, 2012).

is suspicion of control, seek competent help immediately. If it is not nipped in the bud, the control issues will progress and can destroy a relationship. There is nothing as destructive to a relationship as control. Control is trying to exert power over others. Keep this in mind: *Control and love are mutually exclusive.* Control breeds resentment, not love.

There is no life without stress, but we can decide how we react to stress. I try to think, *When I think about this incident five years from now, will I laugh about it or cry over it? If I will laugh at it then, I should start laughing now.*

I was very upset at the airport when my flight was canceled, but I thought as above, that when I think about this in the future, I will laugh at it. All the other passengers were going crazy, yelling at the airline agent as though it were her fault. I was calm, thinking about the future.

My mother used to refer to "*the heilige al tadin,*" by which she meant the statement in *Ethics of the Fathers* (2:5), "Do not judge your fellow until you have reached his place." If you were aware of all the circumstances involved and how they impact that individual, you would judge him favorably or, at the very least, differently. You would want others to give you the benefit of the doubt, so extend the same courtesy to them.

It is so easy to come to wrong conclusions, even when all the evidence appears to justify your conclusion.

I was co-officiating at the funeral of a man who was a member of my congregation and also of another congregation. His funeral was held in the other rabbi's synagogue because it was larger and could accommodate more people.

I knew that the rabbi of the other congregation was not exactly enamored of me. On an earlier occasion, we had appeared together on a panel, and the wit and style of my presentation had upstaged him. He was a good bit older than I, and it was evident that he resented this young upstart.

At the funeral, the host rabbi was first to deliver the eulogy. A few minutes into his address, the public address system failed, and no one beyond the first two rows could hear him. By the time it was my turn to deliver the eulogy, the problem had been corrected, and everyone could hear me.

What if it had been the reverse? What if the public address system had shut down when I was speaking? I would have been absolutely certain that the other rabbi had arranged it so that my speech should not be heard. What could have been more logical than that he did not wish to be upstaged again? No one could have convinced me that this was not deliberate.

Obviously, it *was* an accident, and so are many things that some people may interpret as hostile actions toward them. This experience has enabled me to avoid concluding that I am being maligned.

Even people with perfect hearing can mishear something. Don't jump to conclusions if your husband says something that seems odd or insulting. Ask him to repeat what was said, and then repeat it back to him. This will ensure that what you heard was what he intended.

Both men and women are subject to mood changes. Mood changes can actually be due to subtle chemical changes in the body. However, because women have a physiologic hormonal cycle, they are more prone to heightened mood changes. If these should occur, go for help promptly. There is no reason to suffer unnecessarily.

The most potent ingredient for a lasting, satisfying marriage is *simchah*. It is the responsibility of both husband and wife to make their home a citadel of *simchah*.

When everything goes exactly how one wishes, there is no magic needed to have *simchah*. However, life is full of disappointments, stresses, and challenges, some of which make it difficult to have *simchah*. Rambam says that *simchah* is a requisite for *avodas Hashem* (service of and devotion to G-d). *Avodah* means *work*. Little work is required when circumstances are pleasant. *Avodah* to achieve *simchah* is necessary when conditions are unpleasant.

So many people are searching for the path to happiness, but so few people have found it. Although all Torah writings emphasize the centrality of *simchah* and that Hashem makes His Presence rest where there is *simchah*, it is still a rather rare commodity. This is because we are subject to the influences of our environment, and the prevailing attitude is that happiness is equated with pleasure. Any discomfort, inconvenience, or disappointment results in unhappiness.

We cannot achieve true *simchah* unless we divest ourselves of the prevailing erroneous concept of happiness.

Our problem is that we have bought into the prevailing cultural attitude implying that happiness depends on comfort, convenience, success, and pleasure. When we read what the *sefarim* say about *simchah*, we attempt to apply these teachings without discarding the prevailing cultural attitude. As long as we do this, anything that we may lack in the areas of comfort, convenience, pleasure, and success may make it almost impossible for us to achieve *simchah*.

The Talmud says, "This is the way of Torah: Eat bread with salt, drink water in small measure, sleep on the ground, and live a life of deprivation .... If you do this ... all will be well with you" *(Ethics of the Fathers* 6:4). The Talmud does not mean that we should actually live a life of deprivation. Rather, we *should be able to get along with a minimum*, because then we can be happy with whatever we have. *Luxuries cannot make us happy unless we could have been satisfied without them.*

True happiness and satisfaction in life can be achieved only if we find fulfillment within ourselves. We were indeed created with a physical body that is essentially animal in nature. But whereas an animal need not change its nature and focus only on fulfilling its physical inclinations, we are different. We must become *mentschen*, which means that we must suppress our physicality and live our lives according to the moral teachings of the Torah.

In my book, *Let Us Make Man*,[1] I cited the Baal Shem Tov's comment that when Hashem said, "Let us make man," He was speaking to man. Hashem created angels that are holy and fully spiritual. Hashem's concept of man was that he was to become a spiritual being *by his own effort*. Had man been created fully spiritual, he would have

---

1. *Let Us Make Man: Self-Esteem Through Jewishness* (C.I.S., 1991).

been an angel, not "man." The words "Let us make man" was actually the first mitzvah given to man, to make himself into a *mentsch*.

Unless one makes oneself into a *mentsch*, one is unfulfilled and cannot be truly happy. Indulging in pleasure can produce only a temporary euphoria, much like the addict's experience.

Having a goal in life to experience incidents of temporary euphoria is not the perspective of *Yiddishkeit*. What greater *mentschlich simchah* can there be than the awareness that one has merited the Presence of the *Shechinah*?

The most intense Presence of the *Shechinah* was centered in the *Kodesh HaKodashim*, the Holy of Holies in the Temple, and Hashem spoke to Moses from between the two Cherubim on the Ark. The Talmud says that when the Jews came to Jerusalem on the Festivals, the Kohanim would draw back the curtain of the *Kodesh HaKodashim* and the Jews would see the two Cherubim in an embrace. The Kohanim would say, "See how dear you are to Hashem" (*Yoma* 54a). "When husband and wife have a loving relationship, the Divine Presence is with them" (*Sotah* 17a).

When problems arise in a marriage, there is a tendency to blame one's spouse. But blame never solves a problem. Regardless of who may be at fault, husband and wife should address the problem and try to resolve it. If they cannot do this on their own, they should enlist external help.

An important ingredient for a happy marriage is *hakaras hatov* (lit., recognizing the good). Gratitude is basic to *Yiddishkeit*. We begin the day with *Modeh Ani*, expressing our thanks to Hashem for another day of life. Many times during the day, we recite *berachos*, which are expressions of gratitude. However, sometimes we focus on what we feel we are lacking instead of on the many things we have.

I always thought of myself as being a grateful person. I appreciated what others did for me and I sincerely thanked them. But there was still something about gratitude that I had to learn.

I had just bought a new car, loaded with everything, especially a cruise control. I have a tendency to speed, and I could be speeding without being aware of it. So I use cruise control. For me, that's like Antabuse, the medication that makes you violently ill if you drink alcohol while you are taking it, so it gives alcoholics the control they don't normally have.

Well, my cruise control was not accurate. I would set it at 60 m.p.h. and it would vacillate between 55 and 65. I could have had it fine-tuned, but that would have meant taking the car to the dealer, spending several hours waiting, etc.

I took my frustration to an AA meeting. The speaker was a woman who was telling about the wonderful changes that had occurred since she had stopped drinking. She had obtained a full-time job, and moved to better living quarters for herself and her son. She hoped soon to have enough money to repair her car, which needed a new transmission. The reverse gear did not work, so she had to plan her parking to be able to get out of a parking space without going in reverse. When the audience laughed, she said, "Well, I must remember that some people don't have a car at all."

If I could have dug a deep hole in the ground, I would have jumped in. This woman was grateful that she had a car, albeit without a reverse gear, and here I was griping because the cruise control on my fully loaded new car lacked precision.

Putting matters into the right perspective will engender gratitude. In turn, *simchah* and gratitude will make for a happy marriage.

Of course, life is replete with annoyances and worries, but I learned to have a proper attitude toward them.

When my brother was seriously ill with cancer, I asked a *tzaddik* in Jerusalem to pray for him. As I was about to leave, he said, "May you be blessed with many worries."

Noting my bewildered expression at this strange blessing, he explained, "It is impossible for a human being to be totally free of worry. Ever since Adam and Eve were expelled from the Garden of Eden, man has been subject to worry.

"Sometimes a person has something so serious on his mind that it obliterates all other concerns. For example, you are so worried about your brother's illness that it occupies your entire mind, and you do not pay attention to the myriad of other issues in your life.

"When a person has only one worry, that's bad. It means that there is something so horrific bothering him that he doesn't think of anything else. If one has many worries, it means that there is nothing so overwhelmingly bad that it obscures everything else.

"It is not realistic to be without any worry. That just does not happen. And it is very bad if a person has only one worry. The best situation, therefore, is for a person to have many worries. That means that there is nothing terribly disturbing going on in one's life."

The *tzaddik* continued, "My blessing to you was that you should have many worries. That means that nothing really bad is on your mind."

Now when I find I am worried about half a dozen things, I am happy. Worries are normal, and they should not detract from *simchah*.

There are many things that may call for your attention and effort. We do not have endless time nor do we have limitless energy. We may want to accomplish everything, but this is simply not realistic. We must budget our time and energy just as we do our finances. You may have to set priorities, and this should be done in conjunction with your husband, so that you share both a common end and common means.

My dear granddaughter, don't take a good life for granted. Marriage is a partnership into which each member must invest his/her all. Building a *bayis ne'eman* together with your wonderful *chassan* according to the dictates of the Torah will ensure that the *Shechinah* will dwell in your home.

My *berachah* to you both is that Hashem should further bless you with children and grandchildren who are *lomdei Torah*, *tzaddikim*, and *baalei middos tovos*, and that you and your husband together should merit to greet Mashiach *bimherah b'yameinu*.

To My Great-Grandson, on His Becoming a Bar Mitzvah

My dear great-grandson:

When your father told me that you requested that I write something for your bar mitzvah, I was thrilled. You are fulfilling the final instructions Moses gave to *Klal Yisrael*: "Ask your father and he will relate it to you, your elders and they will tell you" (*Deuteronomy* 32:7). This is a *mitzvah d'Oraisa*, and it is my privilege to respond.

Life is complicated, and there are many challenges one must overcome. Why am I qualified to instruct you? I am not that wise, but what I lack in wisdom, I can compensate for in experience, which, after all, is the best teacher. In addition to the fact that Hashem has blessed me with long life, which, in itself, is a source of experience, I have had fifty years of psychiatric practice, during which I have encountered virtually every problem to which people are susceptible.

I have learned much from these encounters. Like every other human being, I have made mistakes, and I have learned from at least some of them.

We are fortunate to have a wealth of wisdom in our *sefarim* of chassidus and *mussar*, wisdom that is of Divine origin. Although I cannot claim to be a Torah scholar, I did gain numerous precious insights that I will share with you.

The young mind can be very sharp, and one can come to firm conclusions based on superficial observations. However, things are not always what they seem to be, and it requires great skill in discerning what is truth and what is falsehood that masquerades as truth.

When I became a bar mitzvah, the world was much simpler than it is today. Technology has not only revolutionized the way we live, but has also brought about an unprecedented explosion of knowledge. As valuable as knowledge is, there can be an overload; when too much material bombards us, we can become confused rather than wise. We have to pick and choose.

I hope that what I say to you will facilitate your steering a course through life of true *avodas Hashem* and happiness.

You are approaching your thirteenth birthday, your bar mitzvah. This is a momentous occasion, the day on which you will be welcoming a guest that will accompany you throughout your life, the *yetzer tov*. Our Sages tell us that until one is bar mitzvah or bas mitzvah, one is under the influence of only the *yetzer hara*, which is translated as "the evil inclination."

But why is this inclination or instinct called the *yetzer hara*? A tiger is born with the instinct to kill for food. If the tiger kills a gazelle, it is just doing what it was created to do. All living creatures are born with instincts. Why are some human instincts considered *ra*, evil?

This is because a tiger has no other goal that it must achieve. Hashem created it complete with instincts that support its existence. When it kills a gazelle, it is not doing anything that is harmful to itself, but merely seeking sustenance that will ensure its continued survival.

Human beings are different. We were created to fulfill a purpose and a mission in life. We were indeed created with animal-like instincts, but in contrast to the tiger, gratifying some of these instincts can be detrimental, causing us to fail to fulfill that mission and purpose. That is why it is called *yetzer hara*. It is *ra* because it is detrimental.

What is the *yetzer hara*? It is the animalistic drives found in every human being. Giving in to the *yetzer hara* is actually behaving like an animal. It is acceptable for an animal to behave like an animal, but it is not acceptable for a human being to behave like an animal.

Of course, when we are infants, we are unable to tell which actions are harmful. We might touch a hot stove or a sharp knife and suffer a severe burn or a deep cut. We might wander into the street and risk being struck by a car. Our parents try to protect us from harm, but because we lack the ability to understand why things are injurious, we may be angry at our parents for depriving us of things that are harmful. We may want to stay up all night, not realizing that would cause us problems on the following day, and we may be angry at our mother for insisting we go to bed on time.

As we mature and our intelligence increases, we can understand that some things we desire are not good for us. We may wish to eat mushrooms that we have picked while on a picnic in the park, but when our parents tell us that this particular variety of cute red-capped polka-dot mushrooms are extremely poisonous, we defer to their superior knowledge and will discard the mushrooms. When we pass a non-kosher restaurant and beg our mother for a treat, we accept her statement that the food there is forbidden by halachah, and we learn to control our impulses. Because we trust our parents' judgment, we usually obey their injunctions.

However, many of our desires are very powerful, and we may look for ways to justify our obtaining them. Our desires may be so strong that they may influence our thinking, and we actually decide that bad is good and that wrong is right. This is where the *yetzer tov* comes in, to guide us so that we do not make wrong judgments.

Adam was created as a highly spiritual being. When he committed the sin of eating the forbidden fruit, he lost his extraordinary spirituality and was cursed to "eat the grass of the field." The Talmud says that he wept, saying, "Now I and my mule will be eating from the same trough" (*Pesachim* 118a). What he meant was that just as an animal eats to satisfy its hunger, he, too, would function at an animal level, eating only to satisfy his hunger.

This situation changed when we were given the Torah and thereby were enlisted to serve Hashem. This is when our behavior changed from animal/physicality to human/spirituality. We can dedicate our eating to the service of Hashem. Inasmuch as we cannot observe the Torah and mitzvos unless we are healthy and have the necessary energy, we need nutrition, and our eating thus becomes a means to serve Hashem. When we say the *berachos* on food, we are dedicating our eating to the service of Hashem.

This is where Torah and the secular world part ways. The secular world does not see man as having a goal and mission in life. If a person is very intelligent and yet has no goal in life other than comfort and self-gratification, he is really not different from an animal. True, he is an intelligent animal, but an animal nevertheless.

This is why Adam wept when he realized he had lost his great spirituality. Living a Torah life restores our spirituality. The *yetzer hara*, which dominates the animal self, opposes our spirituality because it seeks to bring us down to its level, an animal level.

Hashem, in His infinite wisdom, created many types of creatures. He created angels, pure spiritual beings that have no desire other than to carry out the will of Hashem. He created animals, which have no desire other than to sustain their lives. Then he created man, in many ways an animal-like creature, but He instilled within him a *neshamah* (soul) that would enable him to rise far above the animal level.

You are the bearer of such a *neshamah*. The *yetzer tov*, which you are now acquiring, will guide you to use the virtually unlimited powers of the *neshamah* to break loose from the animalistic drives of the *yetzer hara*. The *yetzer hara* wants to reduce you to living on an animalistic level. You should have too much pride to allow this to happen.

Do not underestimate the powers of the *yetzer hara*. It is very clever and sly, and will stop at nothing to bring you down to its level.

> *The Talmud relates that R' Yehudah HaNasi and Antoninus had a discussion about when the yetzer hara enters a person. R' Yehudah said, "Right from the moment of conception."*
>
> *Antoninus said, "That cannot be. If the fetus had a yetzer hara, it would kick its way out of the mother's womb. The*

yetzer hara does not enter a person until birth."
The Talmud states that R' Yehudah HaNasi conceded
that Antoninus was correct.(Sanhedrin 91b).

The *baalei mussar* ask why the *yetzer hara* would cause the fetus to kick its way out of the womb. What kind of temptations does the fetus have? It knows nothing about worldly pleasures. Furthermore, if it leaves the womb too early, it will die!

They answer that the prime motivation of the *yetzer hara* is not pleasure-seeking. Rather, it is *a rebellion against restriction, confinement, and authority!* The *yetzer hara* wishes to be free of all restraint, and it would cause the fetus to leave the womb and die rather than be restrained and confined.

Remember this. *The yetzer hara is a powerful force that incites you to reject all restrictions and authority.*

In meetings of Alcoholics Anonymous, it is stated that one must be aware that alcohol "is an enemy, cunning, baffling, and powerful." This is an accurate description of the *yetzer hara*.

In earlier times, resisting the *yetzer hara* was not as formidable a challenge as it is today. It was easier to realize that there had to be a goal in life beyond gratifying one's desires. There were so many hardships in life that one could not think that the purpose in life was to live in comfort and enjoy numerous pleasures. When I became bar mitzvah, we had no air-conditioning, no power steering or power brakes, no washers and dryers, no dishwashers, no cell phones, no jet planes, no fax machines, no television, no fast foods, no ready-for-the-pot frozen meals, no electric toothbrushes, no computers, no emails, no microwave ovens. There were no antibiotics. The polio vaccine had not been invented, and every summer we lived through the anxiety of a polio epidemic. I had whooping cough and mumps. There were no school buses, and I walked to school in the below-zero Milwaukee winters.

With all these inconveniences (and more), we did not have as many desires, and we did not feel frustrated when some of our desires were unmet. We could accept that there was something more to life than just having fun.

But your world today is different. Technology has made it possible to live a comfortable life and to indulge in physical pleasures. The *yetzer hara* takes full advantage of this. It tells people that if they are not immersed in pleasure 24/7/365, there is something wrong, and they must do something immediately to correct the situation. The *yetzer hara* pushes the individual to try to "feel good" this very minute, inciting him to long-term self-destructive actions in an attempt to achieve this short-term goal. It encourages one to be totally free to fulfill every desire and not to obey any restrictive authority.

There is yet another social situation that is problematic. On the last day of your twelfth year, you will be a minor all day. When the sun sets on that day, you will undergo a radical transformation. In a matter of a split second, you will become an adult.

This is a very significant *berachah*, because it indicates how halachah and the secular world part ways. In the olden days, the concept of adolescence was unknown. As soon as possible, children were expected to join their parents in the field or home, working alongside them to enable the family to survive. During the Industrial Revolution, even very young children were put to work in factories, often perishing tragically in work-related accidents. Only in relatively modern times have there been enough labor-saving devices and enough leisure time to enable youngsters to enjoy a brief period when they are no longer children without responsibilities and not yet adults when they take on the tasks of work and family. However, this window of lessened responsibility has had an untoward effect on some young adults.

I was once called to the hospital emergency room to see a young man who had come for help. I asked him what his problem was, but he remained silent. I sat with him a few minutes, hoping that he would be comfortable enough to tell me what was bothering him. After a long while, he said, "I am a nothing."

I said, "Why do you say you are a nothing?"

He responded, "What am I? I am not a child, and I am not an adult, so I am a nothing."

I wonder how many adolescents share this feeling.

According to halachah, the father bears the responsibility for the actions of his minor son. When the youngster reaches 13, the father is relieved of this responsibility (hence the *berachah* *"Baruch sheptrani"*) and the young man is responsible for his own actions. *Beis din* will judge the actions of a 13-year-old boy no differently than those of a 40-year-old man. There is not a single moment of lack of accountability.

However, in the secular world, oftentimes adolescents are not held fully responsible for their actions; the adults around them may erroneously fail to demand that the youngsters behave correctly. It is little wonder that so many adolescents engage in destructive behavior since they do not experience consequences when they break laws or express disrespect toward others.

But the damage goes far beyond that. *Once a person experiences a period in which one is not responsible for one's actions, the sensation of responsibility may be defective, and even at the age of 50, the feeling of irresponsibility may linger. Subconsciously, if not consciously, there may be the notion that one can do whatever one pleases, and one is not answerable to anyone for one's behavior.*

So, my dear grandson, do not think of yourself as an adolescent. You are becoming a *gadol*, a full-fledged, responsible adult.

Your challenge in observing Torah is not going to be in keeping the mitzvos. You will put on *tefillin*, observe Shabbos, eat kosher, sit in the *succah*, hear the shofar, and eat matzah on Pesach. Your challenge is going to be in behaving according to the *middos* the Torah requires, because that is where the battleground is with the *yetzer hara*, which wishes to bring you down to an animal level.

The primary characteristic of animal behavior is that it is totally self-centered. Pets can be trained to control their behavior, but the natural state of animals in the wild is that they are totally driven by selfish desires. An animal cannot decide to deny a bodily drive, and it will do what pleases it most. Animals do not have the ability to make choices as to what is right and what is wrong, what is proper and what is improper. As a human being, you do have that ability. If you have a desire to do something that is wrong, you can resist that desire, and that is how you exercise your uniqueness as a human being.

But as noted, the *yetzer hara* is clever and wily. Your *yetzer tov* will tell you that a particular action is wrong, but the *yetzer hara* will tell you that the *yetzer tov* is making a mistake, and will try to convince you that this action is not wrong. It will give you many arguments, some of which may sound very logical. You have to be on your guard not to be taken in by the *yetzer hara's* arguments.

The *yetzer hara* is not stupid. It knows that if it will tell you to do something forbidden on Shabbos or to eat something *tereifeh*, you will not listen. But it may tell you to not be completely truthful about something, and you may find a way of justifying it. Or, if you've heard a piece of gossip, it will tell you to share it with others. The *yetzer tov* may say, "Don't do that! It's *lashon hara!*" but the *yetzer hara* will come up with numerous reasons why it is permissible to tell it. Or, someone may have offended you, and you have the opportunity to get back at him. The *yetzer hara* will tell you that the person is a scoundrel and deserves to be put in his place. The *yetzer tov* will say that taking revenge is forbidden, and that you should forgive him. This is very difficult. *Mesillas Yesharim* says that taking revenge is the sweetest feeling a person may have, and it may take considerable effort to refrain from doing so.

When others have more than you do, it is only natural to be envious, but the *yetzer hara* will say, "You can't control your feelings." The *yetzer tov* will tell you that you must have *emunah* that Hashem is fair, even though some people have more than others. Hashem has a reason for how He runs the world, but our limited human minds cannot grasp His wisdom.

It is virtually impossible to avoid situations that may make you angry. You can't help feeling angry when you're provoked, but you can control how you react to the provocation. Allowing yourself to react in rage is very destructive. The Torah tells us that the great

Moses became angry on only three occasions, and each time he made an error in judgment. The Talmud says that when a person goes into rage, "he is exposed to all the torments of *Gehinnom*" (*Nedarim* 22a). If he is wise, he loses his wisdom, and if he is a prophet, he loses his prophecy (*Pesachim* 66a).

While you cannot avoid feeling angry when provoked, you do have control of how long you want to hold on to the anger. The Torah says we should not hold grudges. Holding on to a grudge makes no sense, because the person at whom you are angry does not care how you feel about him. The only one who is affected by your holding on to a grudge is you, and it can have negative effects on you. It has been said that holding on to a grudge is like swallowing poison and expecting the other person to die as a result of it.

When you say the *Shema* at bedtime, there is a paragraph that reads, "I do not want anyone to be punished because of me." Sometimes, a person who has been hurt by someone else may wish for terrible things to happen to that person. We pray that no person should suffer because of us, and that is a form of forgiveness.

Management of anger is a universal problem, and there are many courses offered on anger management. Our ancestor, R' Nachum of Chernobyl, in *Meor Einayim* suggests a novel approach.

The Baal Shem Tov taught that the world is a mirror. Inasmuch as we tend to deny our character defects and shortcomings, Hashem arranges that we see them in others. "Therefore," said the Baal Shem Tov, "when you see a fault in another person, pause and do a self-search to find where you harbor that very fault."

Based on this principle, *Meor Einayim* writes, when you feel that someone has wronged you, do a self-searching to find *where you have*

— 210 —

acted wrongly toward Hashem. If you will do this, you will be occupied with a soul-searching and you will be critical of yourself rather than of the other person.

Some people, when provoked, will shout or scream. This is a self-destructive mistake. As noted above, when you shout at another person, he tunes you out. He is preoccupied with how he is going to respond to your barrage, and he doesn't even hear what you are saying. If you want to make a point and you want your message to get through, keep your voice soft. King Solomon wrote, "The gentle words of the wise are heard" (*Ecclesiastes* 9:17).

There is a letter the Ramban wrote to his son, cautioning him to avoid rage. It is wise to read this letter regularly.

Beware of the *yetzer hara's* trickery in trying to make you feel inadequate and unworthy. It will say, "What makes you think you can be a *talmid chacham?* What makes you think you can be a *tzaddik?*" You are a precious person with a beautiful *neshamah* which is part of Hashem Himself. You are dear to us and dear to Hashem.

You are going to face challenges in life. *Mesillas Yesharim* says that life is a series of challenges. One can achieve happiness in life, but one cannot avoid challenges.

We cannot understand the wisdom of Hashem. Hashem is infinite, and our minds, however great they may be, are limited. Any effort to understand Hashem is an exercise in futility. All we can know is what Hashem revealed to us in the Torah and through the prophets and the Divinely inspired *tzaddikim*. We know that He wants us to be masters of ourselves and choose to do right.

The Baal Shem Tov noted that in the account of Creation, Hashem created everything by Himself, including everything on earth and all the millions of stars in the galaxies. When it came to the creation of man, Hashem said, "Let us make man." Whose participation was Hashem seeking, and why did He not create man on His own?

All living things were created in a state of completion. Little alligators grow to become big alligators. They do not have to do anything to change from the state in which they were born. Even caterpillars that turn into butterflies after gestating in a chrysalis do not do anything voluntarily to make the change; it happens automatically, programmed in their genes. Angels undergo no changes whatever. They do not even grow.

After creating animals and angels, Hashem chose to create a unique type of creature: one that would be created animal, but with the ability and potential *to turn itself into something almost angelic*, a physical yet spiritual being. This being would be *Man*. Hashem could have created man fully spiritual, but then he would not be Man, but rather simply another angel. Therefore, Hashem sought Man's participation in his own creation. When Hashem said, "Let us make man," He was speaking to man, saying, "I have created you as a physical being, but not just another animal. I have given you the abilities to rise above your physical being and become spiritual. When you do that, you will have become My idea of Man."

Perhaps this is why the Talmud says that when one observes the Torah, that person becomes "a partner to Hashem in the work of creation."

Let us look at the abilities Hashem gave man that distinguish him from other living things.

> Man has the ability to contemplate a goal and purpose for his

existence. I'm sure that animals in the jungle do not think, *What is the purpose of my being in this jungle? What mission do I have to accomplish here?* The ability to contemplate a purpose for one's existence is uniquely human.

➤ Man has the ability to improve, to become a better person. I doubt that any cow in the pasture has ever thought, *What would I have to do to be a better cow than I am?* The ability to improve oneself is a uniquely human trait.

➤ Man has the ability to delay the satisfaction of a desire. He may decide, *Now is not the right time for it. I must postpone it to a later time.* Animals cannot do this.

➤ Man has the ability to defy even a strong bodily urge. He may be very hungry but decides to fast. No animal has ever decided, "*I'm going to fast today.*"

➤ A person may find money that he knows belongs to someone else. He may have a need for money and a strong desire to keep it, but he knows this is wrong. He will overcome his desire and return the money. Animals cannot overcome their instinctual imperatives.

➤ Man can have an urge to take revenge against someone who has offended him, but can restrain himself from doing so. An angry animal will attack an offender.

➤ Man has the ability to do *chesed*, to sacrifice from his personal self and from his belongings to help a stranger. We give *tzeda-kah* to benefit people whom we do not know and will never see. Mother animals care for their cubs, because that is a natural instinct. But they will never leave food for any other hungry animal that is not part of their pack.

> Man has the ability to think about the mistakes he may have made and the wrongs he has done and he can try to compensate for them. Man can do *teshuvah*, animals cannot.

> Man can forgive others. Animals do not have that ability.

> Man can think about the future and make plans for it. Some animals do instinctively store food, but cannot actively plan to deal with the unexpected.

> Man can be humble; although he may be wealthy and powerful, he does not need to feel superior to others and seek to dominate them. Animals do not have humility.

> Man can be considerate and compassionate. Animals in the wild have no such feelings.

> Man can think of and respect his heritage. He can think of the teachings his forebears have transmitted to him, and the great deeds of their lives. Man can appreciate history. Animals do not think of who their ancestors were.

> Man can search for truth. Animals cannot do that.

> Man's curiosity can enable him to discover the hidden secrets of the universe. Animals are limited to the here and now.

All of the above are human abilities. We may implement them or not. We have the ability to be self-aware, but we may not use it. We have the ability to think about a purpose for our existence, but a person may live to be 95 and never give any thought to his purpose on earth. The *yetzer hara* can keep a person completely focused on one's personal needs and desires.

> *A chassid came to the Alter Rebbe and gave him a kvittel (written petition for help or spiritual guidance) in which he listed his many needs. The Alter Rebbe said, "It seems that you have given much attention to your needs. Have you also given attention to why you are needed?"*

We become so preoccupied with our needs that we do not focus on what our purpose is on earth, why we are needed. Perhaps if we gave more thought to what we must accomplish in our lives, our needs would not be as great.

All of the uniquely human abilities listed above have one thing in common: they are not self-centered. As such, the *yetzer hara* resists them all, and tries to distract us with personal desires. It can make some ideas very tempting, but you must realize that in yielding to the *yetzer hara* one is placing in jeopardy all the unique features that give one the distinction of being a human being.

> *A chassid asked his Rebbe for a rule that could guide him in life. The Rebbe said, "The way a tightrope walker keeps his balance is that if he feels himself leaning a bit to one side, he leans a bit to the other side. Inasmuch as most desires emanate from the yetzer hara, when you feel yourself drawn to do something, think of reasons why you should not do it. That way you may retain a balance through life."*

I cannot stress strongly enough the need to develop proper *middos*, because that is our battleground with the *yetzer hara*. Of course, we must adhere closely to the halachos in the *Shulchan Aruch*. However, R' Chaim Vital, successor to the Arizal, says that one must take even greater precaution with *middos* than with the mitzvos and prohibitions. Some people who are extremely stringent regarding the degree of kosher supervision they demand on foods may unfortunately be lax on *middos*.

When I sought guidance from the Steipler Gaon before going to medical school, he advised me to learn at least fifteen minutes of *mussar* every day, and I share this with you. I also urge you to learn *Pirkei Avos* (*Ethics of the Fathers*). It is not enough to read these chapters on Shabbos afternoon in the summer months. You must study them, contemplate them, and digest them. Another profound guide to *middos* is *Proverbs*, learned with a commentary. *Rav Samson Raphael Hirsch on Mishlei* is an excellent commentary.

We had exemplary *middos* teachers in the person of our illustrious *talmidei chachamim* and *tzaddikim*. We are fortunate in having accounts of eminent people and can read about how they lived their lives. They were mortals like you and I, but they dedicated their lives to *avodas Hashem*. Their *kedushah* did not come easily to them. They struggled with many *nisyonos* (spiritual tests) and overcame them. They took literally what we say, *ki heim chayeinu*, Torah is our very life, and they dealt with every element of Torah as if their life depended on it, because they knew it did.

My dear grandson, you are a bright, talented young man, but it is not unusual for people to be unaware of their abilities and skills. The Ramban says that when Moses instructed the people to build the *Mishkan* (Tabernacle), there were items that required special skills. As we know, the curtains of the *Mishkan* were exquisite tapestry, with different patterns on the two sides. For example, one side of the curtain had an eagle, and the other side a lion. This was not embroidered onto the cloth; rather, the images were woven into the fabric. During their enslavement in Egypt, the Israelites worked with bricks and mortar. No one had the fine skills to weave exotic tapestry.

Ramban says that the ability to do this exquisite weaving was not a miracle. Rather, when the Israelites were told what Hashem wanted of them, they were so inspired and enthused that they set out to do it, and *they discovered in themselves these unique skills.*

This is an important teaching. The Israelites were not aware that they had these skills, but their tremendous devotion to do Hashem's will enabled them to discover their hidden talents. According to Ramban, this was a natural rather than a miraculous occurrence. This is true of many people. We would be surprised to know the hidden talents we have. Many people achieve far less than they can.

The key to actualizing our potential is *attitude*. With a positive, enthusiastic attitude we can unlock many skills. The magic attitude is *simchah*.

Chassidic writings are replete with the overwhelming importance of *simchah*. While there are indeed occasions when we celebrate with joy, these are not constant, and yet our *simchah* should be constant.

We recite the *berachah* every morning thanking Hashem for having chosen us from among all the nations in the world to be His children. Our *emunah* in this is adequate reason for *simchah*.

In Shacharis we say, "We are fortunate — how good is our portion, how pleasant our lot, and how beautiful our heritage." Why don't we sing and dance when we say this? How would a person react if he discovered he had the winning ticket to the mega-lottery jackpot? If we can recite these words without feelings of joy, we are *kafui tov*, ingrates.

Many incidents may irritate a person or cause feelings of unpleasantness. Many of these are unavoidable, but we have a choice how to react to them. As I mentioned in the letter to your cousin, a good rule to go by is, "When I think about this incident five years from now, will I laugh about it or will I still be upset? If it's the kind of thing that I will find amusing then, I should laugh about it now."

Many people think, *If only I had more money, a better job, a better house —*, or *If only I could be relieved of my arthritis — then I would be happy.* My many years of experience have taught me that happiness is not dependent on external circumstances. I have seen people actually receive the things that they were sure would bring them happiness, but it just did not happen. True, more money, a better job, and relief from arthritis are pleasant, *but don't confuse pleasantness with happiness!*

R' Samson Raphael Hirsch says that when two Hebrew words are similar, they are somehow related. He points out that *tzomei'ach* (growth) and *same'ach* (happy) are almost identical. This means that *happiness depends on growth.* Our bodily growth stops in late adolescence, but our spiritual growth can continue throughout our entire lives, and when we grow, we can have *simchah.*

You must be extremely careful not to deviate from the truth. The Torah does not prescribe precautionary measures to protect a person from committing sins. These are all of rabbinic origin. For example, the Torah forbids consuming meat that was cooked with milk. The Sages added precautionary measures: we are not to eat meat with dairy even if they were not cooked together. In addition, they restricted eating dairy foods for a period of time after consuming meat. The Torah forbade certain types of actions on Shabbos, and the Sages added a precautionary measure: we are not to handle certain items deemed *muktzeh* (denoting an object that may not be handled, touched, or moved on Shabbos).

There is only one precautionary measure in the Torah itself. In addition to "You shall not lie" (*Leviticus* 19:11), the Torah also prescribes a precautionary measure, "Distance yourself from a false word" (*Exodus* 23:7).

What is meant by "Distance yourself"? If you want to do something, think, *Will I ever have to deny that I did this?* By avoiding acting in a way that you might ever have to deny having done, you are keeping your distance from falsehood.

In the *Shema,* we say, "Hashem, your G-d, is truth." Hashem is identified with truth. If we deviate from truth, we distance ourselves from Hashem.

It is easy to rationalize and justify lying. These rationalizations are the work of the *yetzer hara*. The only permissible lie is in order to preserve *shalom bayis,* peace and harmony between husband and wife. Even then, one must be most cautious not to distort the truth more than is absolutely necessary to preserve *shalom bayis.*

As noted, my mother, your great-great-grandmother, always referred to the "*heilige al tadin,*" by which she meant the mishnah in *Ethics of the Fathers* (2:5) that states, "Do not judge your fellow until you have reached his place." She felt that this was a basic rule in human relations. Sometimes we are quick to criticize a person, but if we were in the same predicament we would understand his behavior.

We want other people to judge us fairly, and we should give them that same consideration.

Furthermore, how we judge others may determine how Hashem judges us. Commenting on the verse in *Psalms* (121:5), "Hashem is your shadow," the Baal Shem Tov stated that just as a person's shadow mimics every movement one makes, so does Hashem act toward us the way we act toward others. If we are quick to forgive others, Hashem forgives us.

There is a beautiful "*Tefillah Kodem HaTefillah* (Prayer before Praying)," composed by R' Elimelech of Lizhensk, in which we pray, "Help us to see the virtues of other people and not their faults." This is a key to happy relationships.

King Solomon writes, "There is no person so wholly righteous on the earth that he [always] does good and never sins" (*Ecclesiastes* 7:20). The Midrash says that *teshuvah* preceded creation of the world. Hashem knew that human beings are prone to making mistakes and doing wrong acts. The world could not exist if there were not a way that a person could correct one's mistakes, but we must understand what true *teshuvah* consists of.

Regretting a wrong act is the first step in *teshuvah*, but is only the first step. Resolving not to repeat the act is an important part of *teshuvah*, but is only a part. True *teshuvah* requires a personality overhaul. Let me explain.

There are things that a truly *frum* person would never do, such as eating *tereifeh* or cooking on Shabbos. These are simply impossible for him to do. However, it is not beyond possibility that he may carry a grudge against someone who offended him, or listen to *lashon hara*.

— 220 —

Although he is aware that the Torah forbids these, they are not in the same league for him as eating *tereifeh* or cooking on Shabbos. If he realizes that he has committed a sin by listening to *lashon hara* or carrying a grudge, it is not enough that he regrets it, and it is not even enough that he resolves that it will not happen again. True *teshuvah* requires that he develop his *yiras Shamayim* to a level where these acts become as impossible for him to do as eating *tereifeh* or cooking on Shabbos.

This is what Rambam says constitutes *teshuvah*. When a person can truthfully say, "I am no longer that person who committed that sin. I have changed. I am a different person." When a person does this kind of *teshuvah*, then the prophet says, "I will have wiped away your willful sins like a thick mist and your transgressions like a cloud" (*Isaiah* 44:22). One should then be secure that Hashem has totally forgiven one's sin.

There are things that happen in the world that we do not understand, especially why bad things happen to good people. Many explanations have been offered, but all fall short of satisfying us. The Talmud says that Moses posed this question to Hashem, and Hashem told him that as long as he inhabits a physical body, he cannot understand this concept. The Talmud says that Moses wrote the Book of *Job*, where various explanations are given for this phenomenon, but all are rebutted. Ultimately, we must have *emunah* that Hashem is just and all that He does is just, even though we are unable to see this from our standpoint.

Like everyone else, I am challenged by things that, to my mind, seem to be grossly unfair, and I am tempted to question Hashem.

In my study, I have a picture of our Zeide Reb Motele, an outstanding *gaon* and *tzaddik*. Zeide Reb Motele was not a mythical figure. I knew Zeide Reb Leibele, who was his son. I knew several of his chassidim. His mind was far, far superior to mine. Every question that I may have was known to him. If he was satisfied with *emunah* in Hashem's justice, that is sufficient for me. People who cannot accept this *emunah* think themselves to be wiser than the Baal Shem Tov, the Vilna Gaon, and the countless great *tzaddikim* of our heritage. I think it is an outrageous chutzpah and an overinflated ego to refuse to accept the *emunah* of these spiritual giants. When I am bothered by a challenge to *emunah,* I look at the picture of Zeide Reb Motele, and my mind is at ease.

I asked a person who had questions in *emunah* how he would feel if he was with a large group of fast-ball pitchers who could throw a ball at 100 miles per hour, whereas he could barely lob a ball 20 feet; would he dare compete with them? That's how one should feel standing in the shadows of our *gedolim.*

Hakaras hatov is a fundamental pillar of *Yiddishkeit.* The Talmud says that one of Moses's sharpest reprimands of the Children of Israel was that they were ingrates (*Avodah Zarah* 5a). R' Chaim Shmulevitz points out that when Hashem told Moses to go to Egypt and deliver the Israelites from their cruel enslavement, Moses said, "I must ask Jethro's permission. He took me in when I was a homeless refugee." But Hashem had ordered him to go free the Israelites from their brutal enslavement! The Egyptians were throwing their infant sons into the river. Was this the time for social niceties? R' Shmulevitz says that Moses knew what Hashem wanted, and that it was Hashem's will that he express his *hakaras hatov* to Jethro.

The word for expressing gratitude is *modeh*, which is also the word for admitting a wrong. It is not a coincidence that the same word applies to both gratitude and admission. The Torah commentaries praise Judah for not denying wrongful behavior (see *Genesis* 38:26). Judah had this trait because his very name in Hebrew, *Yehudah*, expresses gratitude. When he was born, Leah said, "This time let me gratefully praise Hashem" (*Genesis* 29:35). Indeed, the *Chiddushei HaRim* says that Jews have come to be referred to as *Yehudim* (*Megillas Esther* 2:3) because acknowledging and expressing gratitude is a fundamental Jewish trait. Leah engrained in Judah the ability to be *modeh* (grateful), which enabled him to be *modeh* (admit) wrongdoing.

The Midrash says that when Mashiach comes, most of the *korbanos* (sacrificial offerings) will not be brought (because there will be no sins), but the *korban todah*, the offering brought to express gratitude to Hashem, will always be brought.

The *baalei mussar* say that a person who is ungrateful toward other people will ultimately be ungrateful to Hashem.

Gratitude and admission are psychologically related, both being derivatives of self-esteem. A person with low self-esteem may defend his behavior and insist he was right because it is too great an assault to his fragile self-esteem to admit a wrong. Also, *Tosafos* (*Avodah Zarah* 5a) state that the reason the Jews did not want to acknowledge a favor from Hashem is because this would make them feel beholden to Him. A person with proper self-esteem is not threatened by the feeling that he may be indebted to another. Proper self-esteem will enable you to practice *hakaras hatov* and will enable you to admit you were wrong.

Rambam states that all traits have their extremes. A person may be a tightwad or may spend money lavishly and foolishly. A person may be a coward or may be reckless and foolhardy. The proper trait lies somewhere between the two extremes. No extremes are good.

When it comes to halachic issues, of course you must follow the rulings of the Torah, but when you are faced with other personal choices, do not be stubborn and believe, "My way is the only right way. Everyone else is wrong." On the other hand, blindly doing what everyone else wants you to do and not having your own opinion is also wrong. You can listen to various opinions, but don't allow others to decide for you. In forming your opinions, you should be guided by halachah, your parents, and your rebbeim.

It is difficult to go through life without having some resentment toward someone who has offended you. I pointed out that holding a grudge against someone is like swallowing poison and expecting the other person to die from it. The only person who suffers is the person holding the grudge. In addition, you must remember that holding a grudge is a violation of the Torah, which states, "You shall not hate your brother in your heart" (*Leviticus* 19:17). As noted, if you find it difficult to forgive, do what it says in the nighttime *Shema* before bedtime: Pray to Hashem, "Do not let anyone suffer because of me."

When R' Levi Yitzchak of Berditchev was Rav in Minsk,

some of his enemies took his wife and children, put them
on the dung wagon, and sent them out of town. R' Levi
Yitzchak's friends were outraged. They asked R' Wolf of
Zhitomir to punish the scoundrels. R' Wolf said, "I cannot
do anything, because Levi Yitzchak is standing at the aron
kodesh (ark where the Torah Scrolls are kept) saying Tehillim
and praying that no harm come to them."

We are fortunate in having a wealth of *sifrei mussar* that teach us proper behavior and Torah-mandated *middos*. I strongly recommend repeated readings of *Mesillas Yesharim*. For our present generation, *Michtav MeEliyahu* and *Alei Shur* are extremely important.

In *Alei Shur*, R' Shlomo Wolbe presents an essay in which he points out that all human beings are born with a variety of traits, some good and some not good. He says that one should recognize the good *middos* within oneself and seek to reinforce them and improve on them. He says that when a person capitalizes on one's good *middos*, it will help reduce and eliminate the bad *middos* in one's personality.

Think of it this way: A woman sees that one of the chairs in her living room is shabby, and replaces it with a new chair. However, this new chair now stands in sharp contrast to the old sofa, which must be replaced. But now the carpet clashes with the new furniture, and when the new carpet is installed, the drapes are out of sync. Then the lamps and pictures must be brought into harmony. The whole room was beautified all because one chair was replaced.

So it is with *middos*. If one improves a good *middah*, the bad *middos* are incompatible and will be eliminated.

R' Wolbe points out that it is important to avoid knee-jerk reactions.

Knee-jerk reactions are emotionally generated responses that occur without giving thought to one's response. If we think about what we are about to say or do, we are likely to make good judgments. If we act without thinking, we are apt to do something very foolish and harmful. It is natural when provoked to respond in anger, but almost always such a response is wrong and is later regretted. Always think before you act.

There is an important character trait that is often troublesome: *control.* Control often has negative consequences, because people do not like to be controlled, and feeling that control is being imposed on them breeds resentment. This is especially so when control is exercised in a relationship that should be loving, such as between husband and wife or parents and children.

It is understandable that parents must exercise control over an infant who does not have the ability to avoid danger. However, when a child reaches the age of reason, and the parents act in the child's interest, the child can accept the discipline without resentment, and the child will comply with the parents' wishes out of love and respect for the parent.

Many control freaks are people who suffer from low self-esteem, and seek to gain a feeling of self-worth by dominating others. I think this is also true of bullies.

Be extremely careful about the friends you keep. Some friends might be fun to be with, but if their behavior and attitudes are not Torah-inspired, avoid them. They could have a harmful influence on you. Respect your parents' judgment of your friends, and do not associate with friends of whom they disapprove.

The world today is not the world I grew up in. We learn about the sinful cities of Sodom and Gomorrah, whose laws were totally corrupt. Today's society is governed by seeking gratification of one's desires, and if some desires are outlawed, the laws are changed to permit fulfillment of all their desires. It is getting to be like Sodom and Gomorrah. Torah law is eternal. Whatever was forbidden three thousand years ago is still forbidden today.

We refer to the Torah as *Toras Emes*, a Torah of truth. Truth does not change with time. $2 + 2 = 4$, five thousand years ago, and does so today. No congress, no legislature, no court can alter truth, and no one can alter Torah.

My beloved great-grandson, what I am going to say to you now may be difficult for you to grasp, but I am going to say it anyway. You can file it away in your memory, and as you mature and increase your wisdom and understanding, you can give it serious thought.

The human mind has two major components: *intellect and emotions.* We come into the world as a bundle of emotions, or as it is said in *Job* (11:12), "Let him who is born as a wild mule be reborn as a man." At birth we have little or no intelligence. This develops gradually as we grow and mature. We are motivated by our emotions, and *we use our intellect to satisfy our desires.* An infant who sees an object it wants tries to figure out how to get it. This pattern continues to the highest degree of sophistication. All inventions are the result of something we desire. The intellect functions as a tool of the emotions.

In *Tanya*, the Alter Rebbe states that in our spiritual life, the reverse can be true. *The intellect can tell us what we should want.*

A patient who had severe digestive problems was told by his doctor, "You can eat whatever you like; here is a list of what you are going to like." The patient may actually learn to dislike the foods that cause him distress, and he can learn to like the foods that agree with him.

This may be a difficult concept to grasp, and it may take much effort and persistence to achieve, but it is attainable and it is the height of human achievement. Emotions are the animal part of us, and step one of being a human being worthy of that name is to be in control of our emotions. A much more advanced level of humanity is the generation of emotion by intellect.

When you put on the *tefillin*, you say that the *tefillin* headpiece is to devote the *neshamah* in your mind and all your abilities to the service of Hashem, and the arm *tefillin*, which is worn close to the heart, is to subject the desires and ideas of the heart to the service of Hashem. If you are sincere in your intentions, then the power of the mitzvah of *tefillin* will enable you to reach the great achievement of having your intellect generate emotion.

And in closing, my dear great-grandson, let me leave you with a *berachah* that you appreciate the *zechus* you have been granted to be the scion of such an illustrious family, and may you be a source of much true Yiddishe *nachas* to the *Ribbono shel Olam*, *Klal Yisrael*, and your loving parents.

To My Great-Granddaughter, on Her Becoming a Bas Mitzvah

My beloved great-granddaughter:

A year ago, your cousin asked that I write something for his bar mitzvah. I wrote a rather lengthy piece, "To my great-grandson." Now that you are approaching bas mitzvah, I thought I should write something special for you. Actually, much of what I wrote for your cousin is appropriate for you as well.

The fact is that there are not that many differences in *avodas Hashem* between men and women. For reasons known only to Him, Hashem exempted women from time-oriented mitzvos, such as shofar, *tefillin*, and *succah*. Although it is assumed that women are exempt from the mitzvah of studying Torah, that is only partially true.

Men have the mitzvah of studying all aspects of Torah, even those that do not apply to them. Women are exempt from these, but they should learn the halachos of those mitzvos that do apply to them, such as the laws of Shabbos, *Bircas HaMazon*, *tzedakah*, *kibbud av v'eim*, *lashon hara*, *kashrus*, etc.

You might ask why we make a gala event of a bar mitzvah, but bas mitzvah is not given much fanfare in our community. I think that the bar mitzvah ceremony was instituted so that the community should know that this boy is now of age to be counted for a *minyan*, to be called for an *aliyah* to the Torah, and to serve as a *shliach tzibbur*, matters that do not apply to girls. The fanfare of making a party is not a halachah, but a social practice. The party is considered a *seudas mitzvah* only if a Torah discourse is presented.

Following our family tradition, you will begin lighting the Shabbos candles the first Friday evening after your twelfth birthday, and you will recite the *berachah Shehechiyanu*.

There is one all-important aspect of *Yiddishkeit* that applies to women as well as to men, and that is the practice of proper *middos*. My personal belief is that this obligation is of primary importance for women. As mothers, they will have a major impact on their children, who will do as they do — not as they say. As a woman, having exemplary *middos* will make your role as a parent easier and with Hashem's help will ensure *doros yesharim*.

It is unfortunate that some people may be meticulous about observing mitzvos but may be lax in their *middos*. R' Chaim Vital, successor to the Arizal, is emphatic that a person should be *more* cautious and meticulous about *middos* than about both positive and prohibitive mitzvos (*Shaar HaKedushah* 20). Some people who are very stringent, for example, with regard to drinking only *chalav Yisrael* and eating only *pas yashan*, may not be as careful about losing their temper, holding a grudge, or other character traits. According to R' Chaim Vital, this is a perversion of *Yiddishkeit.*

The *baalei mussar* explain that although committing an *aveirah* is most serious, nevertheless, it is an isolated event and does not become part of one's personality. One can, therefore, more readily do *teshuvah.* A bad *middah*, however, tends to become engrained in one's personality, and it is much more difficult to uproot it.

While observance of all mitzvos is of greatest importance, Moses stressed *yiras Hashem, ahavas Hashem,* and *middos* as precursors to performing mitzvos. "Now, O Israel, what does Hashem, your G-d, ask of you? Only to fear Hashem, your G-d, to go in all His ways (*middos tovos*) and to love Him, and to serve Hashem, your G-d, with all your heart and with all your soul...." Only in the next verse does he say, "... to observe the commandments of Hashem and His decrees" (*Deuteronomy* 10:12-13). This does not detract from the importance of mitzvos, but it does set the priorities.

> *The Talmud relates that the students of Rabban Yochanan ben Zakkai visited him shortly before his death and asked for his blessing. Rabban Yochanan said, "May your fear of Hashem be as great as your fear of human beings" (Berachos 28b). People will avoid doing wrong if they are afraid others will notice them, but are not afraid to do these acts in privacy, clearly not concerned that Hashem sees them.*

There is thus a serious lack of *yiras Shamayim* in some people who observe mitzvos. Moses's priority was correct.

I believe that the role of the mother in teaching proper *middos* is actually greater than that of the father. King Solomon writes, "Hear, my child, the discipline of your father, and do not forsake the teaching of your mother" (*Proverbs* 1:8). King Solomon is very precise with his words. He says that you should listen to your father to *acquire* his teaching, but in regard to the teaching of the mother he says, *do not forsake it*. In other words, at the time you reach the age of reason, the teaching of your mother is something *you already have*, so make sure to retain it.

The major transmission of *middos* is not didactic, but rather heart to heart, by interaction and nonverbal communication. In the early years of life, the child is primarily in the company of the mother, and it is from her that the child absorbs *middos*. When the child reaches the age of reason, King Solomon instructs him to listen and *acquire* what his father teaches him, but he does not have to *acquire* his mother's teachings. These were already implanted in him, and he must simply be careful not to stray from them.

And so, my dear granddaughter, as a future mother, you must give much attention to perfecting your *middos,* because you will be transmitting these to future generations.

In the discussion of *middos,* I will follow the format of Ramban in his famous *Letter to His Son*, which begins with the instruction to avoid *kaas* (anger).

One of the most difficult emotions to manage is anger. *Chazal* condemn anger in the sharpest terms: "If one is in anger, it is equivalent to idolatry" (Rambam, *Hilchos Dei'os* 2), and "If one is in anger, all the forces of *Gehinnom* overtake him," and "If one is in anger, if he is a prophet, he loses his prophecy, and if he is wise, he loses his wisdom" (*Pesachim* 66a). No other emotion is dealt with as harshly. The Talmud points out that Moses became angry on only three occasions, and each time, he erred in halachah (*Vayikra Rabbah* 13). Indeed, Rambam says that it was because Moses reacted angrily to the people's demand for water that he was denied his one fervent wish — to enter Eretz Yisrael.

It is important to clarify terms to avoid confusion. Rambam's ruling that *anger* is equivalent to idolatry is not found anywhere in the Talmud. Rather, the Talmud says that if a person breaks things or tears his garments in a fit of anger, it is equivalent to idolatry (*Shabbos* 105b), and this is what Rambam is referring to, rather than the "feeling" of anger.

The confusion arises because the same Hebrew word is used for three distinct phases of anger. The first phase is the *feeling* a person has when offended, and this is referred to as *kaas*. The second phase is the reaction one has; i.e., how one behaves when one feels angry. This, too, is referred to as *kaas*. The third phase is holding a grudge or resentment, retaining the anger after the provocation is over, and this, too, is referred to as *kaas*. It is extremely important to distinguish between these three phases.

The pure feeling of anger when one is harmed or otherwise offended is not within one's control. After all, our physical body is essentially an animal body, and has all the animalistic emotions. In davening we say, "The superiority of man over animal is nonexistent, except for the pure *neshamah*." In other words, we come into the world with animalistic drives, and by invoking the power of the *neshamah*, we can gain control over these drives, and we may even be able to convert them and channel them to constructive expression.

It is known that the Chofetz Chaim would come into the *beis midrash* after midnight, open the *aron kodesh*, and pray tearfully that Hashem should relieve him of the feeling of anger. No one ever saw the Chofetz Chaim react angrily, because he was in total control of his behavior. However, our inborn feelings are not under our control, and we may not be able to rid ourselves of them. Therefore, the Chofetz Chaim asked Hashem to take away this objectionable feeling.

In some cases, it may indeed be possible to avoid even feeling angry when provoked, but this may not apply to all provocations.

The Talmud is very clear in stating that it is when a person reacts to anger by breaking things or tearing his garments that it is equivalent to idolatry, not when he *feels* anger on provocation. Rambam, then, is using the word *kaas* in the sense of *rage* in his ruling. If a person reacts with rage, this is indeed wrong and one must learn to avoid this. However, a person need not feel guilty for having felt anger when provoked, because this is not under one's voluntary control. When Ramban, in the letter to his son, tells him to avoid anger, he is referring to *rage*, the reaction to anger.

It is of interest that Ramban tells his son that by avoiding rage, he can achieve *anivus* (humility), which is the finest of all *middos*. The obvious question is, why doesn't he begin by telling his son to develop *anivus*, rather than telling him to avoid rage, which will then lead to *anivus*?

Ramban understood human nature. You can tell a person what *to do*, but you cannot tell a person what *to feel*. We must find ways to develop proper feelings. They cannot be ordered.

Therefore, Ramban instructs his son to avoid rage. Whereas one cannot control the *feeling* of anger, one can control one's reaction. A person can avoid a rage reaction.

Certain feelings are incompatible with other feelings. When a person succeeds in subduing rage, the attitude of arrogance (*ga'avah*) is now incompatible with his character; hence he can develop *anivus*.

A derivative of *kaas* is *nekamah* (revenge). The desire to "get back" at someone who has offended you is extremely strong. Ramchal in *Mesillas Yesharim* says that taking revenge is "sweeter than honey" and may be the only thing that will give a person peace of mind. It would seem that restraining oneself from taking revenge is something that could be demanded of angels rather than of human beings. Yet the Torah does demand it of us, and we must rise to the challenge.

Another negative *middah* that one must overcome is *envy*. If your neighbor trades his car for a new one every two years, while your car spends more time in the repair shop than in your driveway, it is very difficult not to be envious. You can be envious of another student who has better grades or who comes from a wealthy family and can afford things that you cannot afford. Every day, in the "*Tefillah Kodem HaTefillah*" of R' Elimelech of Lizhensk, I ask Hashem to protect me from envy. Envy is such a worthless feeling. All it does is cause distress. It never gets you what you want.

R' Mendel of Rimanov says that Hashem gave the Israelites the manna before giving them the Torah, because the manna taught them that Hashem will provide for them exactly what they need. If they gathered more than their share of manna, it spoiled. If they gathered less than their share, the container filled itself. It is only with true *emunah*, believing that Hashem provides everyone with their needs, that one can observe the many halachos that restrict us from improper self-enrichment. If we can believe that Hashem provides us with our needs, we can avoid envy.

You have the precious gift of youth. Be careful not to lose it.

As noted above, the Maggid of Mezeritch said that there are three things we should learn from babies:

1. A baby is always happy.

2. A baby is never idle.

3. When a baby wants something, it cries for it.

I believe that the first two are related. The reason a baby is always happy is *because* it is never idle. The baby is curious about the world, and will crawl over things and under things because it wants to find what is there. As we grow older, we lose our curiosity and consequently our motivation. There is so much to learn, so much that we do not know but could know, that we should never be idle. If we will constantly learn, we will be happy. When you're young, you're excited about learning new skills and absorbing new information. Don't lose this excitement.

One of the most important *middos* is *hakaras hatov*, expression of gratitude. It would seem that this should be an easy *middah* to achieve, but it is not always so. Moses chastised the Israelites for their being ingrates. Tosafos say that they did not want to feel gratitude to Hashem because it would make them feel obligated to Him, and they did not want to feel obligated (*Avodah Zarah* 5a). The reason we have so many *berachos* is because we should be thankful to Hashem for everything, great or small.

Kavod habriyos, respect for people, is a fundamental *middah*. The Talmud says that the great Rabban Yochanan ben Zakkai would be the first to greet everyone he met in the street, even non-Jews.

Emes (truth) is more than just a *middah*. We say, "*Hashem Elokeichem emes*, Hashem *is* truth*." *Midvar sheker tirchak*, which literally means *distance yourself from falsehood*, also means that falsehood causes one to distance oneself from Hashem. We often try to justify twisting the truth. This is a serious mistake.

We often rationalize twisting the truth, and we may justify "white lies." Children are "color blind." If they detect your "white lie," it will become a green light for them to lie as well.

I know that I do not have to impress upon you the importance of *tzniyus* (modesty). There are halachos that regulate *tzniyus*. People may set more stringent standards for *tzniyus*, and they mistakenly believe that anyone who does not live up to that standard, even if she is dressed according to halachah, is lacking in *frumkeit* (piety).

> *R' Velvele of Brisk was known to be a very strict machmir (one who is stringent concerning halachah). One Succos someone saw him drinking coffee in his house, and was clearly surprised. He said, "The Rav is machmir on so many things,*

yet the Shulchan Aruch states that although one is permitted to drink outside of the succah, a person who is machmir not to drink outside of the succah is praiseworthy."

The Brisker Rav said, "Is that what they say about me, that I am a machmir? That is not true. When there are varying opinions regarding any given situation, I must take precautions not to violate halachah according to any authorities. But here everyone agrees that the halachah is that one may drink outside of the succah, but that a machmir is praiseworthy. Well, I am not a machmir on actions that are unquestionably permitted by halachah."

Tzniyus is not restricted to the length of a garment. If clothes are ostentatious or if one flaunts one's jewelry, that's a violation of *tzniyus*.

It is possible that there will be times when you will have questions. So many things occur that seem unfair to us, and no amount of arguments can satisfy us. I am not immune to such thoughts and doubts. As I wrote to your cousins, when these thoughts and doubts occur, I look at the picture of our Zeide Reb Motele. He was an outstanding *gaon* and *tzaddik* and was far, far smarter than I am. Any questions that I may have are certainly known to him. If his *emunah* in Hashem and in His justice was firm, there is no reason for me to second-guess him.

Throughout our history, we had spiritual giants who towered over us. Their unshaken *emunah* is enough to set my mind at ease.

Bitachon (trust in Hashem; feeling secure in Hashem) is a fundamental *middah* in *Yiddishkeit*. Some people think that *bitachon* means feeling confident that when you ask Hashem for something, you will get it. The Chazon Ish said that this is incorrect. There may be reasons why Hashem will not give us what we request. A person may ask for something he thinks is good for him, but Hashem knows otherwise.

The Talmud says that in Heaven, the Gates of Tears are never closed (*Berachos* 32b). One of the chassidic masters rhetorically asked, "If these gates are never closed, then what is the purpose of having a gate?" He answered, "If a person cries like a fool, the gates are shut."

> *The Chofetz Chaim asked a person how he was faring, and the man said, "Things could be better." The Chofetz Chaim said, "What makes you think things could be better?"*

The Midrash says that when Joseph was taken from him, Jacob said, "Hashem has turned away from me." Hashem said, "I am arranging matters to make his son viceroy of the greatest empire in the world, and he is complaining" (*Bereishis Rabbah* 91:1).

The Chazon Ish said that *bitachon* means to be secure in the conviction that Hashem is fully in charge of everything in the world and conducts the world in the way His wisdom knows is best (*Emunah U'Bitachon*).

Zerizus (diligence; alacrity) is an extremely important *middah* and is actually the key to a successful life. In *Effective Living*,[1] I quoted Ramchal in *Mesillas Yesharim*, who says of procrastination that "*ein sakanah kesakanto* (there is no danger as great as its danger)." If a person

1. *Effective Living* (Shaar Press, 2014).

decides that he will not do something, his decision may be right or wrong, but he is not deceiving himself. However, if he says, "I will do it, but just not right now," he is deceiving himself. The truth is that he really does not wish nor intend to do it, but does not admit it to himself. Lying to oneself is always destructive.

One may procrastinate because of laziness, or one may procrastinate because one is afraid of failure and wishes to escape this eventuality. King Solomon devoted much of *Proverbs* to the problems of indolence and procrastination.

The Torah represents the Divine wisdom. This holds true for the *Chumash* (Five Books of Moses), the Books of the Prophets, the Talmud, and for the works of the great Torah scholars. We cannot always appreciate the great wisdom in every word of Torah. However, we can easily appreciate the wisdom of the "wisest man in the world," King Solomon, in *Proverbs*. I urge you to study *Proverbs*.

Our society is said to be suffering from "affluenza," the disorder resulting from affluence. As you know, much of my psychiatric practice has been treating alcoholics and addicts. The prime characteristic in these conditions is that the addict is never satisfied. His body builds up a tolerance to the chemical so that whatever he consumes is not enough.

When I was a child, my mother used to tell me bedtime stories. One of them was about a poor man who prayed that he should become wealthy. One morning, upon awakening, he found a purse near his bed. The purse contained a dollar, and when he removed the dollar, another dollar appeared in its place. Three days later, he was found lying dead atop a pile of dollars.

I had no way of knowing when I was 5 years old that this is the story of addiction. One needs more and more and pays for it with one's very life.

But addiction is not the only time when this occurs. Many people are not satisfied with what they have, constantly looking for thrills in new acquisitions. Be careful. It is easy to fall into this trap. We all have "wants" and "needs." We must be careful that our wants not become needs.

After the Holocaust, some of the survivors reached Israel (which was then Palestine) with nothing but the clothes they were wearing. Our shul took up a collection of used clothing, and I made it into bundles and sent them off.

One day we received a "thank you" letter from one of the people who had received the clothing, and it was written on personalized stationery. I showed it to my father, expressing my wonderment how a person who depends on used clothing can afford personalized stationery. My father explained that this person was a member of a very wealthy family. To her, personalized stationery was not a luxury, but an essential of life, much like food and water.

Be careful that you do not allow your "wants" to become "needs." Living an austere life can prevent becoming infected with "affluenza."

There are some people who are chronically dissatisfied with life, and are constantly looking to make meaningless changes in their lives in the hope of finding happiness.

My beloved great-granddaughter, know that the future lies in your hands. Try to emulate your *chashuve* mother and grandmothers and grow up to be a true *Yiddishe Mamme*. Your davening, especially those *tefillos* where you shed heartfelt tears in beseeching Hashem to grant *berachah* and *hatzlachah* to you and your offspring, can be most powerful. Turn to Hashem with all your needs and wishes. He is a loving Father Who wants only the best for His children. May He fulfill all your prayers for good.

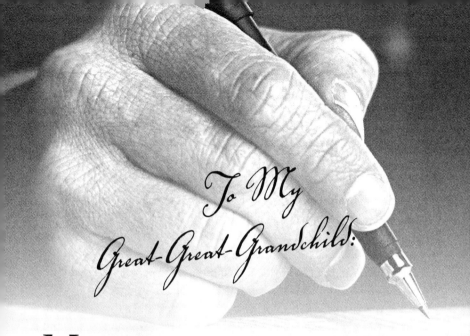

To My
Great-Great-Grandchild:

My beloved great-great-grandchild:
   I am writing this to you, even though you have not yet been born. I follow the precedent of Moshe Rabbeinu, who said that he was making a covenant with as yet unborn generations (*Deuteronomy* 29:13).

   Although you are as of now unknown to me, I owe you a great debt of gratitude. There is a tradition that if a person lives to see a fifth generation, he will be spared the ordeal of *Gehinnom*. Thus, this is an invaluable gift you are giving me.

   I have no idea what the world you will live in will be like. I have seen the world undergo very radical changes in my lifetime. No one in the 1930's could have imagined what life would be like in the twenty-first century. Many laws and practices that existed in the 1930's are no longer extant. How then, do I presume to give you guidance for the world in which you will be living, which is totally unknown to me?

Moshe Rabbeinu made the covenant more than three thousand years ago, and it is still valid, regardless of the changes the world has undergone since then. This is because Torah is eternal, and its laws do not change. The halachos that were given when people traveled by ox-cart are still in effect when we travel by jet.

Some people may excuse their actions by saying, "Of course, I would be more observant of Torah if I had a spiritual leader like the sages of the Talmud, or like Rashi, or like the Baal Shem Tov, or like the Vilna Gaon." That is a cop-out. There were people in those days who did not observe Torah, and there are people today who do observe Torah.

I regret that you do not have a great-grandfather like I had. You will read about our Zeide Reb Motele, who was a great *gaon* and *tzaddik*. Although I did not know him personally, he, along with the other great *tzaddikim*, serves as a guide for me.

We have a sense of right and wrong and justice. When we see things happening that we think are unfair and unjust, we may ask, "Why does Hashem allow such things to happen?"

When we ask such questions, we are in good company, because the Talmud says that Moshe Rabbeinu himself posed this question to Hashem. "Why are there *tzaddikim* who suffer, and why are there *reshaim* who prosper?" The Talmud says that Hashem told Moshe Rabbeinu that this is beyond comprehension (*Berachos* 8a).

What we must understand is the caliber of our *tzaddikim*. The immensity of their Torah knowledge and wisdom, and the level of perfection of their *middos*, are far beyond ours. Every possible question that we may have about how and why Hashem conducts the world has certainly occurred to them. These questions did not affect their *emunah* in Hashem and should not affect ours.

As I wrote to your older cousins, there was a picture of Zeide Reb Motele in my father's study, and I have that picture in my study, too. Whenever I am bothered by questions of *emunah*, I look at that picture and realize that if Zeide Reb Motele was secure in *emunah*, that's good enough for me. I suspect that this picture in my father's study served the same purpose for him. People constantly came to him, sharing their problems and *tzaros*. I think he used this picture for *chizuk*.

Jews in Russia had even greater *tzaros* than we do, and they poured out their hearts to Zeide Reb Motele. On one occasion, when the suffering of the Jews was more than he could tolerate, he pulled open his shirt and said, "*Ribbono shel Olam!* Look into my heart! I cannot take any more pain!" Nevertheless, he continued to be a source of comfort to those who consulted him, and his *emunah* did not falter.

The Torah says, "Do not perform the practice of the land of Egypt in which you dwelled, and do not perform the practice of the land of Canaan to which I bring you" (*Leviticus* 18:3). The Torah has clearly specified 248 mitzvos that we must perform, and 365 prohibited acts that we may not perform. What is the Torah referring to when mentioning avoiding the practices of the Egyptians and Canaanites?

The Torah refers to lifestyles and standards of right and wrong, good and evil. The secular world has standards that are unacceptable to Jews. People think that those who have a great deal of money are wealthy, that he who can exert the greatest power is strong, that those who can expound much knowledge are wise, and that those who receive the greatest acclaim are the most honored. Torah standards are different. The Talmud says, "Who is wise? One who learns from every person. Who is wealthy? One who is satisfied with whatever he has. Who is strong? One who can be master over himself, and not yield to his desires. Who is honorable? One who respects others" (*Ethics of the Fathers* 4:1).

We are always at the risk of being influenced by our environment. The Torah is telling us to be on our guard to avoid adopting those ethical and moral standards found in our environment that may be detrimental to our *neshamos*.

Many people believe that if a person observes all the mitzvos and avoids transgressing the prohibitions, one is fulfilling one's Torah obligations. Ramban says that this is not so. A person may be in technical compliance with all the mitzvos, yet may be an unrefined, vulgar person. *Ethics of the Fathers* and the chassidic and *mussar* literature tell us what it takes to truly be observant of Torah.

A great source of teaching is the lives of our *tzaddikim*. We have such accounts, many of which are your ancestors, and we can learn from them what is required if one is to follow the way of Hashem. As a child, I thrived on the stories that I heard from my father and others, and that I read in reliable biographies of the *tzaddikim*. Let them be your guides, as they were mine.

I want to share with you a basic concept of *Yiddishkeit* that is not stressed enough. We say *Shema Yisrael*, and we are told to have *kavannah* to accept *ol malchus Shamayim*. The word *ol* is extremely important. *Ol* means a yoke, the wooden frame that is put on the neck of the ox when plowing. The yoke does not permit the ox to stray from the path on which the farmer directs it.

As intelligent people, we want to understand why we must do certain things. Certainly we want to understand Torah to the degree that we are able, but we must remember that Torah reflects the infinite wisdom of Hashem, and what we understand is just a tiny crumb of infinity. We must accept Torah as an *ol*, a yoke that guides us on the proper path in life.

You are, *baruch Hashem*, very bright, and it is only natural that you want to understand everything you do. King Solomon was the wisest of all men, and his *Sefer Mishlei* (*Book of Proverbs*) is a great source of wisdom. This great wise person says, "Do not rely on your own understanding" (*Proverbs* 3:5). *Kabbalas ol* is the foundation of *Yiddishkeit*, and will lead you to the correct path in life.